WITH HIS HAND

The Incredible Story of John C. "Red" Morgan

WITH
HIS HAND

A story of the incredible experiences
of B-17 pilot John C. "Red" Morgan
during World War II

Daniel Simmons

LUMINARE PRESS
WWW.LUMINAREPRESS.COM

With His Hand: The Incredible Story of John C. "Red" Morgan
© 2018 Daniel Simmons

Printed in the United States of America
Cover photos courtesy of Irving Baum and Sam Morgan
Cover concept by George Cardenas, Springfield, Oregon
Cover design by Claire Flint Last

Luminare Press
438 Charnelton St., Suite 101
Eugene, OR 97401
www.luminarepress.com

LCCN: 2018956468
ISBN: 978-1-64388-015-0

This book is dedicated to

Leroy S. "Stan" Williams, Major, USAF, Retired,

who is another one of my American military aviator heroes.

It is also dedicated to my family:

Wendi, Danielle, Julie, Peri, Cyrus, Chris and Zak.

TABLE OF CONTENTS

CHAPTER 1

Early Life

From the day he was born, John Cary Morgan appeared to be in a battle against death. Morgan, known for most of his life as "Red" because of the color of his hair, would win that battle time and time again against all odds. Born in Vernon, Texas, on August 24, 1914, and weighing only two and one-half pounds (his sister claimed it was closer to four pounds), Red almost didn't make it through his first day. A premature birth was a serious issue in 1914. In Red's case, the attending medical personnel believed that he did not survive the birth and placed him aside to concentrate on his mother who was hemorrhaging. When the nurse returned to Red, she discovered he was indeed alive but not doing particularly well. In the early 20th century, incubators in small towns like Vernon were rare. The nurse placed him in a laundry basket under electric lights and surrounded him with hot water bottles. Although Red would survive this brush with death, he had no idea he would somehow miraculously survive three closer calls later in life on board a B-17 during WW II, earning the Distinguished Flying Cross in the first, the Medal of

Honor in the second, and becoming a prisoner of war in the third. As Red's sister Mary Tom would tell him later in life, he had been born with a guardian angel on one shoulder and a little devil on the other. "They were pointing to each other and saying, 'You take him; I don't want him. He's too much of a challenge.' Well, the angel lost out and had to guard him for 75 challenging years."

Red was the son of attorney Samuel Asa Leland (S.A.L.) Morgan and Verna Johnson Morgan. The Morgans had two more children while living in Vernon—daughters Sarah ("Sally") Evelyn and Mary Tom. In 1918, when Red was 4, the family moved from Vernon to Wichita Falls where S.A.L. continued his work as an attorney. Wichita Falls was also the home to much of Red's extended family at the time, with three of his aunts being teachers in the city's school system.

It wasn't long before S.A.L.'s focus turned from Wichita Falls to a city in the panhandle that was becoming a boomtown after the discovery of oil and gas. Amarillo seemed like a desirable place to live, work, and play, and S.A.L. began exploring his options in the panhandle area. In 1922 he bought a 22.5 section ranch with the headquarters located near Texline, 120 miles northwest of Amarillo. The Morgans remained in Wichita Falls at first, but began spending summers at the ranch, taking two days to make the 400-mile trip on mostly unpaved roads at the time. In 1926 S.A.L. packed up the family and moved to Amarillo, settling in a house on the corner of 20th and Washington Streets. Although Red lived in Vernon and Wichita Falls, and spent considerable time at the Texline ranch, it was Amarillo he would call his hometown long after he left Texas.

When Red was small, nobody in his family could ever imagine him growing up to become one of our nation's greatest WW II flying heroes. To say he was a mischievous youngster would probably be a gross understatement, at least according to his younger sister Mary Tom. In Mary Tom's account of Red's early days, she gives a number of examples of how Red tormented siblings, parents, teachers and just about anyone with whom he came in contact.

Mary Tom described Red as having an "impish grin" when he was a young boy, apparently unable to conceal his playful and often bedeviling nature. There were many stories from the summers spent at the ranch near Texline. The ranch had twelve working cowboys, and Red liked hanging out with them even though he was less than ten years old. When he wasn't riding his horse, Red enjoyed the cowboys' lessons in driving a car and rolling cigarettes.

Red had his share of memorable incidents on the ranch, including falling off his horse, getting his foot stuck in the stirrup and being dragged across the ground. In Mary Tom's account of her brother's escapades, it appeared she particularly enjoyed telling the story about hot metal that became lodged in Red's boot. He was rolling a piece of lead across the top of the hot coal stove in the kitchen when it fell off into his boot. He had custom-made boots that were difficult to remove, not ideal when a scorching piece of lead is stuck inside. Mary Tom recalls, "Being kids, my sister Sally and I were laughing at John's dancing around and yelling, but we finally got the boot off. However, I'm sure that John had a scar on the top of his foot the rest of his life." He also relished in antics such as putting snakes in the silverware drawer, a prank not appreciated by his mother who would sometimes accompany the kids to the ranch. Red always seemed to enjoy his time on the ranch with his sisters and later with young brother Sal, Jr. ("Sam") as well.

When Red attended Wolflin Elementary School in Amarillo, he became a handful for the principal, Ethel Jackson. While most students were afraid of Jackson, Red was not one of them. He loved to entertain his classmates and was not thwarted by spankings from the principal, nor by follow-on punishment at home after the principal notified S.A.L. With Red's grandfather and seven aunts still living in Wichita Falls, the children would often return there for visits. They had free passes to ride on the train from Amarillo because S.A.L. was the local attorney for the Burlington railroad line. Mary Tom recalled one return trip from Wichita Falls in 1926 where the children met a prominent lady from Amarillo—Mrs. Allen Early, Sr.—and her children. As the oldest, Red was responsible for Sally and Mary Tom and wanted to make a good impression on Mrs. Early. Making sure the grand lady from Amarillo was watching, Red offered his sisters some gum which they accepted. As soon as Mrs. Early was no longer watching, "John started to choke us and say 'give me my gum back.' We did and he added it to the wad he already had in his mouth." Mary Tom continued that "For years every time I happened to see Mrs. Early she commented on what a little gentleman John was and how responsible he was. I always agreed and said 'YESS, ma'am.' "

II

S.A.L. WAS CONTINUALLY FRUSTRATED WITH HIS OLDEST son's lack of focus in school. During one summer, he sent Red off to Cheley Camp for Boys in Colorado. Frank H. Cheley founded the camp, located in Rocky Mountain National Park 75 miles northwest of Denver, with the goal of helping boys grow into manhood in the great outdoors. This seemed like a perfect place for Red to mature and maybe settle down a bit. This never happened though, and Red continued to fight the attempts to educate him back in Texas. There was one amusing story from Cheley Camp, however, that involved a portrait of Red sketched by a "starving artist" in camp. When Red returned home from camp he tossed the crumpled portrait at his mother saying, "Some artist gave me this and told me to bring it to you." The "starving artist" was Grant Wood, who later became famous for the universally recognizable "American Gothic" painting, depicting a farmer holding a pitchfork with his daughter by his side.

Red's struggles with his schooling would continue throughout his young life. Not happy with his Amarillo schools, he would return to Wichita Falls on occasion to live with his aunts and attend school there. Although several Wichita Falls newspaper articles credited him with attending Zundelowitz Junior High, the only official record from the Wichita Falls Independent School District shows him attending high school there from 1928 to 1929. The issue with Red was not that he wasn't intelligent; in today's vernacular we would probably say he didn't apply himself. S.A.L. tried to get him to do his homework by isolating him in the dining room, only to discover later that Red had been spending his study time drawing scores of pictures of the popular comic strip character Barney Google. In August of 1930, S.A.L. sent Red to New Mexico Military Institute in Roswell, New Mexico, in hopes that the challenging military environment would be a good fit. Although Red was not a star student by any means, he did manage to graduate from high school there in May 1932. After graduation and unsure of what to do next, Red spent a portion of the next year enrolled at Schreiner Institute, a junior college and military school located in Kerrville, Texas. Then in 1934 he attended one semester at the University of Texas in Austin, but he really had no intention of attending any of the classes there. At this point in his life he had decided what he wanted to do; he wanted to fly.

As a young boy in North Texas, Red would see the barnstorming pilots swoop low overhead and was fascinated by the thought of flying. He recalled the first time he saw an aircraft was when he was in Vernon, just short of his 4th birthday. He and his father were outside talking to their neighbor. "I heard this ungodly noise up in the air. I had no idea what it was. I looked up and here is this black thing flying. From that point on I craved nothing but flying." He had his first airplane ride at the age of 7, flying out of Call Field near Wichita Falls, and the dream developed further. Despite his less-than-stellar academic performance in school, he never lost focus on the idea of someday becoming a pilot. He had his first flying lessons at English Field in Amarillo, and while S.A.L. thought his son was getting a college education at the University of Texas in 1934, Red was taking more flying lessons instead. "I was always at the airport," said Red. He soloed after only three and one-half hours of flying. S.A.L. considered his son's flying ambition to be "foolish, impractical and dangerous."

When Red went off to the University, S.A.L. basically gave him blank checks to write as needed for his education and for "pocket money." S.A.L. threatened to cut off that pocket money if his son didn't quit flying in "old crates that were tied together with wire." One day S.A.L. showed up unannounced at Red's apartment, confronted him, and asked if he was gambling because he had cashed so many checks. Red confessed that he was not gambling but rather spending the money on flying lessons. Red related that his dad would probably have been happier if he had been gambling instead. "He probably wished I had been gambling because he thought I was going to get killed." S.A.L. cut off his "allowance" and made him leave the apartment to go into a boarding house where for $22 a month he would get room and board and that was it. "I was starving to death," said Red. His father's disapproval did not deter Red, however, and he devised some unconventional and even unscrupulous ways to pursue his dream. According to the account by Mary Tom, near the end of his semester at the University of Texas, Red sent a wire to S.A.L. saying "Am in the hospital with a ruptured appendix. Send money." A ruptured appendix was a serious medical issue in 1934. Unbeknownst to Red, his father boarded a plane to fly to Austin to check on his seriously ill son. When S.A.L. arrived he visited every hospital in the city but couldn't find Red. He then went to Red's residence where his roommate told him that not only was Red not in a hospital, he was out taking a flying lesson! It was at this point that S.A.L. gave up on the idea of a college education for his son. "I'm through. You're on your own from now on."

In an interview Red did just before he died, he talked about his father and the relationship between the two. S.A.L. always wanted Red to be an attorney like him; Red knew that would never happen. Despite their differences Red always respected and loved his father, and there were never any serious conflicts between the two. In reflecting back, Red managed a big smile when relating his father's reasoning for not wanting him to pursue an aviation career. As an attorney, S.A.L. would often have to fly to the West Coast, and he actually had great respect for the pilots. According to Red, "Dad thought the men flying the airplanes were geniuses for getting him safely to his destinations. He questioned in his mind whether or not I was a genius." He continued, "I think he thought I was a nut. And he was right!" Red also told the story of his father when S.A.L. was approaching the end of his life. S.A.L. was well liked and had many visitors during his final days. While Dad was on his deathbed, "he had the most fun telling stories about me." The love, admiration and respect were clearly mutual between the attorney and the pilot, between father and son.

III

OUT OF SCHOOL AND OUT OF MONEY, RED DID HAVE A RATHER exciting option available while he temporarily set aside his goal to become a pilot. One of his aunts had married a Brit who owned pineapple plantations in the Fiji Islands. With no better plan available at the time, Red headed off to Fiji to work in his uncle's pineapple fields. Not always happy with the working arrangements on the plantations, he also spent time on the islands working in newly discovered gold mines there. His reputation as a reckless youth continued on Fiji with an account of him driving a car and being involved in a head-on collision. As the story goes, there was only one road around the island and only two vehicles, yet somehow Red managed to hit the other one. The big redhead always said the story was false, claiming there was only one vehicle on the island. In any event, the legend of Red lived on, long after he left the islands three years later. According to Mary Tom, when her brother left Fiji, island natives lined the roadside waving and yelling "good-bye Big Red."

Back in Amarillo in 1937, Red began to try out the local job opportunities, including work at a carbon black plant and then as an oil rig roughneck. In 1939 he began what would eventually become a 40-year relationship with Texaco, when he moved to Oklahoma City to become a tank truck driver for the oil company's bulk station there. It was in this job that an incident would occur that would impact his dream of flying at least in the short term. Although he had previously worked as a roughneck in Amarillo, as it turned out his neck was not rough enough. One day while loading a 50-gallon drum of oil onto a truck, he used his neck as a lever and cracked a vertebra. Although the results were not as serious as they could have been, Red was identified as having broken his neck. This injury meant that he was labeled as being unfit for military service (a classification known as "4-F"). With the war looming in Europe and the chance of the U.S. becoming involved, Red was devastated that the injury would prevent him from contributing as a pilot. Despite what seemed like insurmountable odds, Red was not going to give up on his dream.

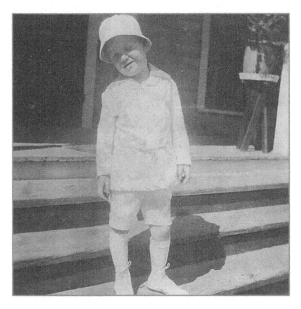

Young Red in Texas. Courtesy of Sam Morgan

The young scholar. Courtesy of Sam Morgan

Sophomore in High School. Courtesy of Sam Morgan

Daniel Simmons

CHAPTER 2

Off to War

In 1940, with it appearing more likely the U.S. would become involved in the war in Europe, Red once again tried to join the U.S. Army Air Forces. Once again he was denied, not only for his neck injury but also for his poor academic record. His lack of focus on his education had come back to haunt him. It appears, however, that a good academic record would not have helped him anyway; the fact he was classified 4-F still remained the real showstopper.

Red's dad, S.A.L., was always a great letter writer. He continuously kept his sisters informed of what was happening in the family and particularly with Red. Maybe it was because he was an attorney, but he seemed to have a gift of putting words to paper. As Red was weighing his options about the future, S.A.L. penned a letter to his sisters addressing the deteriorating situation in Europe and how it would impact not only Red but his brother Sam as well.

If the country becomes involved in a war of defense, I would expect him (Red) to enter the army when others similarly situated are called on to go. I don't think he will rush in as a matter of mere adventure. Had he been able to go on and qualify as an expert aviator, he might do so, just because of his love for that kind of thing; but I do not expect him to rush in just for the thrill of getting into uniform. He got over a lot of that walking area down at N.M.M.I. (New Mexico Military Institute). A uniform probably doesn't appeal to him as much as it would to one who had never worn one. Naturally, I am depressed when I think of the direction in which we are going because of these two boys, both of whom would doubtless be called on should this country become involved in a serious war.

Regarding the uniform issue, S.A.L. had no idea that his son was indeed considering wearing a uniform again, but not one worn by the U.S. military forces.

When Red was in Oklahoma City he married a fellow redhead, a woman named Wilma, and he began discussing with her the idea of going to Canada to try and join their air force. This idea did not go over well with Wilma, but Red kept pursuing that possibility. Despite fierce objections from his wife, Red picked flying over his wife and decided to go north. His decision led to a divorce, but Red believed this was his only chance to get into the war as a pilot.

II

The Canadians never asked Red about his medical issues, and somehow he never managed to mention that he was classified 4-F by the U.S. military. Red had a number of letters of reference for the Canadians, primarily from S.A.L.'s friends. The letters included accolades such as "very energetic and industrious, will not hesitate to devote himself untiringly to the duties assigned him, properly reared, comes of a fine family, habits and character are above reproach and is a young man of excellent moral principles." With England heavily involved in the war against Germany, the Royal Air Force (RAF) was in desperate need of pilots, and the Royal Canadian Air Force (RCAF) was an important source for the Brits' military aviators. The Canadian official who interviewed Red documented that he was "A good average. Older than usual age and basic training evident. Good appearance. Large build physically. Appears straightforward and intelligent. Appears keen. Good material." The Canadians were more than happy to accept the strapping 26-year-old, six-foot redheaded man from Amarillo.

On July 27, 1941, S.A.L. drove Red to Windsor, Ontario, where the young Texan was promptly accepted as a candidate for a pilot's commission with the rank of sergeant-pilot. Red's determination to become a pilot was finally in his grasp, and he was not going to let go of it. On the first of August he officially attested (took his oath of allegiance) and became a member of the RCAF.

In an update letter to his sisters, S.A.L. wrote:

> *John has joined the Canadian Air Force...He is taking a very serious step...He just couldn't see going into one of these draftees' camps as a private and spending an indefinite period marching around through the mud or dust and carrying a rifle or a broomstick and going through the same calisthenics through which he went for 3 ½ years in military school. You probably know that he has done a lot of amateur flying. That experience*

together with his military training ought to put him in line to make rapid progress toward his commission.

Red's training would take him across Canada, beginning in Brandon and Dauphin in Manitoba. He then moved on to Regina in Saskatchewan before returning to Manitoba, spending time at Virden before going back to Brandon. His final training stop would be in Hagersville, Ontario.

Red trained in a British-built Vickers Wellington, a two-engine long range medium bomber, affectionately known as the "Wimpy." Red confessed that it took the Canadians a long time to train him as a military pilot. With all of the personal flying he had done, his critique of himself suggested the skills didn't translate well in the RCAF. Red was probably just being hard on himself. His RCAF training records indicate he did just fine, grading his qualification as "Satisfactory" and his conduct and character as "Very Good."

Throughout his training in Canada, Red held out hopes of flying fighter aircraft. When the RCAF told him this would not happen, he was very disappointed. In February, during a break in training, Red visited S.A.L. and Verna, who now lived in New York City. He shared his feelings about wanting to fly single-seat fighters rather than the bombers. He wanted to be responsible for his life only—he was concerned about the thought of being responsible for the lives of the other crew members on board a bomber. In the back of his mind he was probably thinking of his reckless behavior as a youth, and he didn't want his actions to jeopardize anybody else.

While in New York, Red met a major from the U.S. Army Air Forces who advised him the bomber mission, not the fighter mission, was the key to winning the war. The fighters were just escorts while the bombers were doing the real work against the enemy. Regarding Red's concerns about being responsible for other crew members, the major told him this was actually a good thing, that bomber pilots were more careful knowing other lives were at stake. This exchange was helpful for Red, and the only remaining fear he had was the Canadians would keep him on as an instructor rather than sending him overseas. Fortunately for Red, this did not happen. On October 9, 1942, Red received his pilot wings and the RCAF designated him for assignment to England. The long, difficult journey to become a combat pilot had come to an end.

III

ON OCTOBER 24, RED ARRIVED IN HALIFAX, NOVA SCOTIA, and three days later boarded the RMS *Queen Elizabeth* for the long, slow crossing of the North Atlantic to England. The converted luxury liner arrived in England on November 11, where Red entered the process of officially transferring from the RCAF to the RAF. Almost immediately, Red began looking into the possibility of transferring to the American forces, who he knew were on their way over to join the fight. Red would fly combat missions with the Brits, flying Halifax and Lancaster bombers, but his time with the RAF would be very brief. On March 23, 1943, the RAF transferred Red to the 92nd Bombardment Group (92 BG) of the 8th Air Force (8 AF) of the United States Army Air Forces (USAAF). According to Red, the U.S. paid $50,000 to the RAF to get him. As it would turn out, it was a great bargain buy.

Canadian Pilot. Courtesy of Sam Morgan

Daniel Simmons

Red at RCAF Dauphin, Oct 1941.
Courtesy of Sam Morgan

Red with RCAF friends—Red always on the far left.
Courtesy of Sam Morgan

Daniel Simmons

CHAPTER 3

A U.S. B-17 Pilot

I

Red was very happy to move from the RAF to the USAAF. The U.S. was paying its pilots $225 per month while the Brits were paying only 9 pounds (roughly $36) every two weeks. And after all, he was an American. He wanted to be flying for the U.S. from the start. His rank with the RCAF and RAF had been a sergeant pilot, but the U.S. designated him a flight officer—a warrant officer not yet commissioned. He would not receive his commission as a second lieutenant until later in his tour with the 92nd. When Red transferred from the Brits, the USAAF in England was not aware of his broken neck and 4-F classification. At this point they didn't really care anyway; they were happy to receive an experienced pilot. While many U.S. pilots were arriving into the European theater straight out of pilot training with approximately 200 flying hours, Red had already accumulated over 800 hours with his civilian and RCAF/RAF military flying time. Even with all of his flying experience, he was still going to start out as a copilot of a B-17 Flying Fortress in the 92 BG.

The 92 BG, comprised of four B-17 squadrons, had

already established a reputation as a premier flying group in the 8 AF. Activated on March 1, 1942, the 92nd was the first 8 AF organization to fly non-stop by squadrons across the North Atlantic, deploying from Gander, Newfoundland, to Prestwick, Scotland, in August 1942. Later that month, the unit moved from Scotland to its first operational base at RAF Bovingdon in Hertfordshire, England. After flying four combat missions from Bovingdon, the 92nd was removed from operational missions to become the Combat Crew Replacement Center for 8 AF, responsible for facilitating the combat readiness of new B-17 personnel arriving into the European theater. In January 1943, most of the group departed for its new station at RAF Alconbury in Cambridgeshire. It was here at Alconbury where Red would join up with the 92nd, the unit that would come to be known as "Fame's Favored Few." Nobody would gain more fame in the 92nd Bombardment Group than one John Cary Morgan from Amarillo, Texas. Red would end up flying only five sorties with the 92nd, but two of them would be quite eventful, to put it mildly.

B-17 Copilot with the 92nd Bombardment Group.
Courtesy of Sam Morgan

II

IN THE SUMMER OF 1943 THE ALLIED COMBINED BOMBER Offensive was in full swing. The Allied plan called for the USAAF to bomb targets during the day and the RAF to bomb at night. Daylight precision bombing was the mission of the 8 AF and therefore the mission of the 92 BG. American and British planners agreed on four priority targets: 1) U-boat building facilities, 2) aircraft production plants, 3) ball bearing plants, and 4) oil refineries. Other important targets included harbors and coastal airfields.

On July 4, 1943, the U.S. Bomber Command in Europe directed the 92 BG, along with other B-17 groups, to bomb the aircraft factory at Chateau Bougon near Nantes in Nazi-occupied France. The German Luftwaffe was using the airfield there to launch attacks against targets in England. Of the 124 aircraft dispatched on this mission, the 92nd launched 16 B-17s from RAF Alconbury.

Red was the copilot on a crew led by First Lieutenant Robert L. Campbell of Liberty, Mississippi, the command pilot for this mission. The B-17 had a total of 10 crew members, including the two pilots, navigator, bombardier, flight engineer/top turret gunner, radio operator, and four more gunners—ball turret, tail, left waist and right waist. The navigator and bombardier stations were below and forward of the pilots in the nose of the aircraft, the flight engineer/ top turret gunner was above and behind the pilots, the ball turret gunner was in an isolated position underneath, and the remainder of the crew was in the back of the aircraft.

Besides Red and Campbell, the other crew members on this mission included Navigator Henry A. Hughes Jr., Bombardier Robert S. Wilkins, Flight Engineer/Top Turret Gunner Tyre C. Weaver Jr., Radio Operator Glen E. Johnson, Ball Turret Gunner Richard O. Gettys, Tail Gunner John C. Ford, Left Waist Gunner Reece Walton and Right Waist Gunner Eugene F. Ponte. It was common practice for crews to assign a name to their assigned aircraft, and this B-17 had the name *Ruthie,* named for Campbell's girlfriend.

L/R B/R Combs, Reese, Walton, Gettles, Ford, Weaver
F/R Wilkens, Campbell, Hughes, Red Morgan
Courtesy of Gene Ponte

Photo showing most of the crew members who flew on
Ruthie *on July 4, 1943*

The mission that day was actually a three-pronged attack. While the 92 BG's element was to bomb Nance, another element of the B-17s had Le Mans as its target while the third had La Pallice. It was only recently that the USAAF had begun sending escort fighters to accompany the B-17s across the English Channel. At the time, the P-47 Thunderbolt was the best high-altitude fighter plane the U.S. had. Although effective against German fighter aircraft, the P-47 had limited range and was unable to escort the bombers to and from the target areas. The German Luftwaffe understood this and would routinely delay their attacks on the B-17 formations until after the P-47s turned back.

As the 92 BG formation approached Paris, following the departure of the friendly fighter escorts, one of the elements broke off to the left to proceed to its target at Le Mans while the 92nd continued south to Nantes. As the 92nd approached the initial point on its bomb run, it didn't take long for the

German Focke-Wulf (Fw) 190 and Messerschmitt (Me) 109 fighter aircraft to zero in on the formation. Dozens of fighters, mostly Fw 190s, attacked from above and behind the formation. The attack was furious, with enemy fighters passing on both sides of the formation as well as underneath. The air battle was so intense and so continuous the B-17 crews were unable to recall specific details of each attack after they returned from the mission. Couple this vicious fighter attack with flak from the ground being fired over Nantes, to say the least, it was a trying time for the bomber crews to complete their mission.

In the cockpit of *Ruthie* the pilots focused on the bomb run. In the back of the aircraft the gunners were trying desperately to save the B-17 from the relentless fighter attack. Since *Ruthie* was at the end of the formation, it was an easy target for the German pilots attacking from the rear. As Red's aircraft approached the target, the Fw 190s began to hit hard. Ponte, the right waist gunner, remembers seeing the number 4 engine being hit, followed by the flames shooting past his window all the way to the tail section. At about the same time, Gettys was hit as the German 20-millimeter (20 mm) shells tore into the B-17. Gettys was seriously wounded, and his screams could be heard throughout the aircraft. Despite the intense pain, he valiantly kept firing his guns until he passed out.

Seeing that the engine fire was out of control and burning furiously, Weaver jumped out of his position and raced to the cockpit. He pulled the throttle out of Campbell's hand to shut off the fuel that was feeding the fire. Although the fire went out, the dead engine began to vibrate so hard Ponte thought it would break off of the wing. The enemy fighters sensed the kill and began to swarm around the stricken *Ruthie*, attacking in formations of three to five abreast from the rear of the aircraft. Crew members did not know the fate of Ford, the tail gunner in the back, wondering how he could survive the onslaught. Walton's gun had jammed, so he went to the ball turret to check on Gettys. After moving the wounded gunner out of his position and making him as comfortable as possible, Walton returned to his gun while Hughes tended to Gettys' wounds. Walton's gun was still jammed, and according to Ponte, he just shook the malfunctioning weapon at attacking fighters while screaming choice words at them.

Ruthie managed to stay airborne as it tried to make it home but continued to take massive hits from the enemy aircraft. Two engines were now out, two gas tanks were punctured, and the fuselage was riddled with 20 mm cannon fire. Back over the English Channel, Campbell and Morgan descended to protect the belly of the aircraft since the ball turret gun on the bottom of the B-17 was inactive as a result of Gettys' injuries. The crew saw most of the fighters turn back as *Ruthie* made its dash for the English coast. However, just as the crew members began to think the worst was over, they saw two German Junker (Ju) 88 aircraft approaching quickly from the rear, "coming to finish us off." With all of *Ruthie's* remaining 50 caliber guns blazing and the B-17 dropping violently towards the water, the Ju 88s missed completely. Weaver, with a bird's eye view from the top turret, saw a stream of cannon fire go over his head, "which surely would have blown us out of the sky."

III

WITH THE ENEMY THREAT GONE, THE EMERGENCY WAS FAR from over. Nobody on the crew knew whether *Ruthie* was going to make it to landfall, let alone back to their home field at Alconbury. The gunners were all huddled in the radio room preparing for either a water landing or a crash landing on the coast. It was clear to Campbell and Morgan they would have to find a suitable landing area very quickly where they would try to put the B-17 safely down. RAF Portreath was on the far southwest tip of England and offered the crew a viable landing strip. As *Ruthie* approached the coast, the crew discovered the hydraulics were out. This meant one of the crew members would have to manually lower the landing gear and flaps.

As Campbell and Morgan struggled to maintain control of the bomber, Weaver raised the floor plate to gain access to the manual cranks and lowered the landing gear. He was still straining to lower the flaps when *Ruthie* hit the ground on the runway at Portreath. Upon touchdown, it was apparent the left tire was flat, resulting in a rough ride down the runway and causing the B-17 to veer off of the runway. When the uncontrollable aircraft finally came to rest near the control tower, the crew immediately picked up Gettys and carried him out the rear exit door to awaiting medical personnel. Tail Gunner John Ford, whose fate was unknown after the vicious rear assaults, did receive leg wounds but was not seriously injured. Both Ford and Gettys would recover from their injuries. *Ruthie*, on the other hand, was not so lucky.

The valiant B-17 that brought all crew members safely home had sustained such severe damage that it never left RAF Portreath. *Ruthie* would never fly again, becoming a source of scrap parts for other aircraft. Besides the aforementioned engine, gas tank and hydraulic issues, the tail section was badly damaged, one of the wing's ailerons was blown apart, and the entire airframe was riddled with holes. It was something of a miracle that the bomber was able to stay in the air.

In an interview after the mission, Campbell said, "I thought all the time I was going to have to ditch the ship." He also stated that Red was instrumental in getting the aircraft safely on the ground. "The controls were so tough coming home that Copilot Morgan pulled some tendons in his shoulder helping to hold them."

Red would receive the Distinguished Flying Cross for his actions during this mission and probably thought the sortie was a once-in-a-lifetime unbelievable story of survival. SA.L. probably believed the same. In a letter to his sister, S.A.L. wrote about Red's mission saying, "Of course I am filled with pride for the part he played in this heroic feat; but my chief happiness is in the fact that he escaped with his life from the very precarious situation in which those boys were placed." Neither Red nor his father realized the July 4 mission would pale in comparison to what the young Texan would face three weeks later.

Ruthie *would never fly again. Courtesy of Sam Morgan*

Flattened tire

Damaged tail section

Daniel Simmons

Bullet-riddled airframe

CHAPTER 4

Earning the
Medal of Honor

I

It is hard to imagine a more harrowing flight than what Red experienced on July 4. Despite the narrow escape, his crew was back in action almost immediately, continuing to be tasked for missions over mainland Europe. July 26 would be Red's fifth mission with the 92 BG, and the day started as any other in theater, with the crew eating breakfast and attending the morning mission briefing.[1] The target on this day was Germany's large Continental Vahrenwald tire factory in Hanover. With their B-17 no longer flyable after the July 4 mission, the crew had a new aircraft, named *Ruthie II*. Campbell was still Red's pilot in command, but there were many changes in the composition of the crew from the one that flew the July 4 mission. On this sortie the navigator was 2nd Lt Keith Koske from Milwaukee, Wisconsin, and the bombardier was 2nd Lt Asa J. Irwin from Portland, Oregon. The radio operator was TSgt John A. McClure from Atlanta,

---

1   Some later accounts would incorrectly report the date as July 28

Georgia, the ball turret gunner was SSgt James L. Ford from Chicago, Illinois, and the tail gunner was SSgt John E. Foley from Portland, Oregon. Besides Campbell and Morgan, the only crew members from the July 4 mission were waist gunners Walton, from Joplin, Missouri; Ponte, from St Louis, Missouri; and Weaver, from Riverview, Alabama.

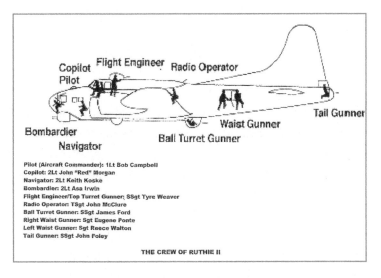

Copilot Flight Engineer Radio Operator
Pilot

Tail Gunner
Bombardier   Waist Gunner
Navigator   Ball Turret Gunner

Pilot (Aircraft Commander): 1Lt Bob Campbell
Copilot: 2Lt John "Red" Morgan
Navigator: 2Lt Keith Koske
Bombardier: 2Lt Asa Irwin
Flight Engineer/Top Turret Gunner: SSgt Tyre Weaver
Radio Operator: TSgt John McClure
Ball Turret Gunner: SSgt James Ford
Right Waist Gunner: Sgt Eugene Ponte
Left Waist Gunner: Sgt Reece Walton
Tail Gunner: SSgt John Foley

THE CREW OF RUTHIE II

The 92 BG was sending 19 aircraft to Hanover, with *Ruthie II* flying the left wing position of the high squadron in the formation. Departure from Alconbury and formation join-up was relatively routine, and the B-17 group headed out over the English Channel enroute to Germany. British Spitfire fighters escorted the bombers at first, but like the American P-47 fighter aircraft, the Spitfire did not have the range to continue providing protection over mainland Europe. As the formation approached the mainland, the escorts turned around. It was not long after this that the German fighters pounced on the 92 BG bombers. *Ruthie II* was approximately 10 miles off the coast when an estimated 150 enemy aircraft—

Me 109s and Fw 190s—attacked.

From his copilot seat on the right side of the aircraft, Red immediately saw in front of him the German fighter aircraft that would change his life forever. Several Fw 190s were headed straight for the *Ruthie II*, coming in at high speed from a position a little high and slightly right of the nose of the aircraft (Red reported it as being from the one to two o'clock position). The German pilots began firing their 20 mm cannons, with shells piercing the cockpit of *Ruthie II*. Red was not sure which Fw 190 in the attacking group hit the *Ruthie II*, but one of them did, and it was with devastating effectiveness. In one burst from the enemy fighter, the first 20 mm shell smashed through Red's windshield, passed in front of his face and hit Campbell on the right side of his head. Red looked over and saw that the side of Campbell's head was blown off and his brain was hanging out. At the same time, a second shell came through Red's side window, passed once again in front of him, and exited the left side of the aircraft. The third shell went behind Red's head and hit his top turret gunner, Tyre Weaver. Another shell entered the cockpit and detonated, shattering the instrument panel.

While the cockpit was receiving devastating fire, the rest of *Ruthie II* was hit hard as well. Shells tore through the length of the fuselage, hitting critical life-supporting systems in the rear of the aircraft. The attack took out the interphone system and the oxygen supply source for the gunners, oxygen being critical for survival of crew members at high altitude. At this point it seemed like the *Ruthie II* was not likely to survive this onslaught from the German attack.

In the now blood-splattered cockpit, the gruesome wound to Campbell did not kill him. Inexplicably, Campbell was somehow able to function and continued to fight, instinctively grabbing the control column and fighting to maintain control of the aircraft. Red, realizing his pilot was gravely injured and unable to fly the B-17, attempted to wrest control from Campbell. At this point, Campbell was in a crazed condition, unwilling to give up command of his aircraft. Red fought to get him off of the controls so he could try to get *Ruthie II* stabilized and keep the aircraft in the formation for protection from further attacks. Campbell wrapped his arms around the controls and would not let loose, thrashing at Red and throwing violent punches at his desperate copilot.

The situation behind the pilots was equally grim. The third shell from the Fw 190 hit the top turret gunner, Tyre Weaver, at the shoulder, completely severing his left arm from his body. Weaver, bleeding profusely, fell out of his position and slumped to the floor just behind navigator Koske's station. Behind Koske and Weaver, the gunners in the back faced a totally different, but equally critical situation. With the loss of oxygen at 24,000 feet, one by one the gunners began losing consciousness. Not knowing the interphone was also out, Walton attempted to contact the pilots to tell them to descend or everybody in back would die from lack of oxygen. Even if the interphone was working, the pilots would not have heard them, since one was critically wounded and the other was fighting to keep the B-17 in the air.

In his injury-induced crazed condition, Campbell continued to struggle with the controls, causing *Ruthie II* to begin falling out of the formation. Red continued to fight him because Campbell's actions were making the B-17 descend to lower altitude, out of the protection of the formation. With Campbell punching Red with one hand and keeping his other arm wrapped around the control column, *Ruthie II* was in desperate trouble. Red continued to battle Campbell, trying to bring the B-17 back into the formation. With his left hand he held off Campbell while using his right hand to fly the bomber. He tucked *Ruthie II* under the aircraft in front of him, looking up to maintain position while continuing the mission. He knew if the *Ruthie II* left the formation, she would be a sitting duck for the German fighters.

------------------------------ **II** ------------------------------

DOWN BELOW, IN THE FRONT OF THE AIRCRAFT, BOMBARdier Asa Irwin was firing the nose guns at the German fighters and preparing for the bomb run. He had no idea what was going on in the other compartments of the aircraft. He was simply focused on protecting the aircraft and getting his bombs on target. He was doing the job he was trained for. In the bottom of the aircraft, Ford was in his ball turret position, isolated from the rest of the aircraft and crew. Because this position had an oxygen supply separate from the gunners in the rear and his oxygen was still flowing, Ford was also busy trying to protect *Ruthie II.*

Behind the pilots, the situation with Weaver was critical. When Koske got to the gunner, he saw his left arm had been blown off at the shoulder, and he was a mass of blood. Koske tried to inject some morphine, but the needle was bent and he could not get it in. The navigator's first thought was to stop his loss of blood. He tried to apply a tourniquet, but it was impossible because the arm was off so close to the shoulder. Koske knew he couldn't save Weaver because the crew still had four hours flying time before landing back in England. Weaver would not survive this flight if he stayed on board.

In the rear of the aircraft, nobody was conscious due to lack of oxygen. With the crew members unconscious in the back, the guns quit firing. Red, not hearing anybody on interphone and the guns not firing, believed they had all bailed out from the crippled aircraft. With the gunners in back not firing and Weaver severely wounded, the only guns working in the *Ruthie II* were being manned by Irwin in the nose and Ford in the ball turret.

While all of this was going on, Red continued to battle Campbell, and *Ruthie II* kept moving ahead with the formation, now approaching Hanover and the target area. Koske knew there was nothing he could do for Weaver, realizing the gunner needed urgent medical attention. The young navigator knew the only hope for Weaver was to have him bail out, where hopefully he would receive medical treatment from the Germans. *Ruthie II* was only 25 miles from Hanover, and the Germans were about to receive an American willingly dropped from a B-17.

According to Koske's personal account, "I opened the escape hatch and adjusted his chute for him. After I adjusted his chute and placed the ripcord ring firmly in his right hand, he must have become excited and pulled the cord, opening the pilot chute in the up draft. I managed to gather it together and tuck it under his right arm, got him into a crouched position with legs through hatch…and toppled him out into space." Koske's hope was that Weaver would be found and given medical attention immediately. From his ball turret position, Ford would later report that he saw Weaver's chute open.

Now over Hanover, the target area was a mass of smoke, but Irwin, seemingly still unaware of the crisis in the cockpit, was able to drop the bombs from *Ruthie II*. The mission was complete; the question now is whether the crew and aircraft would make it home.

FLAK BURSTS AND THE ONGOING ATTACKS FROM GERMAN fighters continued to pummel the formation as it turned around for the trip home. Red continued to fight Campbell for control of *Ruthie II* and thought about ripping the oxygen mask off of his pilot's face, thinking he would become unconscious and the immediate crisis would be over. Red didn't do it, fearing the action would certainly kill his aircraft commander, who was also his good friend. Believing that the crew members in back had already bailed out, he also considered doing the same. Once again, he rejected that option, not wanting to leave the aircraft with anybody still alive remaining on board.

With Koske's ordeal involving Weaver over, he attempted to contact the pilots over the interphone with no success. According to Koske, it did not seem as if anything was terribly wrong up front. "Except for what I thought to be some violent evasive action, we seemed to be flying okay." It was two hours after the initial attack, when the *Ruthie II* was 15 minutes out from the English Channel, that Koske decided to go up front and check on the pilots. What he saw was a horrific scene. Campbell was slumped down in his seat in a mass of blood with the back of his head blown off. In what can only be described as unbelievable and unfathomable, Red had held off the battling pilot with his left hand while flying the aircraft with his right for over two hours—completing the bomb run and now trying to make it back to England.

The 20 mm shell that hit Campbell had virtually shattered the windshield in front of Red, making it impossible for him to see forward. With no forward vision, there was no way he could land the aircraft from his copilot seat. He immediately told Koske they had to get Campbell out of his seat so Red could move over and make the landing from the pilot's position. Just like everything else on this mission, this was not an easy task. According to Koske, "Morgan and I struggled for 30 minutes getting the…injured pilot out of his seat and down into the rear of the navigator's compartment, where the bombardier held him from slipping out the open hatch. Morgan was operating the controls with one hand and helping me handle the pilot with the other."

As *Ruthie II* crossed the English Channel, Red began a descent, looking for the nearest airfield to put down the crippled B-17. The aircraft was dangerously low on fuel, and the crew would find out later that the tanks had been hit, causing a significant fuel loss. In addition, the fighter attacks had rendered the hydraulic system inoperative. Even without these mechanical problems, Red had no plans to make it back to Alconbury, realizing that Campbell needed immediate medical attention if he had any chance to survive. During the descent, as the aircraft dropped from the oxygen-depleted altitude, the crew members in back began to regain consciousness. Miraculously, the loss of oxygen for so long did not kill them, and they began to assist the other crew members in preparation for landing.

Now flying from Campbell's seat, Red decided to land at RAF Foulsham in Norfolk County. With the hydraulic system out, crew members had to manually lower the flaps and landing gear. In addition to all of the other problems, the B-17's radio had been damaged and nobody on *Ruthie II* was able to contact the control tower. With no instructions from the tower, Red had to find an opening in the traffic pattern to safely position his aircraft for a safe landing. The crew fired a flare on the approach to the airfield, notifying ground personnel of the need for a medical response. After the harrowing mission, the landing was rather uneventful, and medical personnel immediately met the aircraft to tend to Campbell. It had been four hours since the initial devastating attack until *Ruthie II* landed. Unbelievably, Campbell was still alive and continued his violent fight for survival. When the crew lowered the wounded pilot out of *Ruthie II* to the waiting doctor, Campbell pulled his legs up and kicked the doctor in the chest, knocking him back 20 feet. The ambulance rushed Campbell from the airfield, but he would succumb to his wound within an hour after the landing.

The crew found out later that Tyre Weaver had indeed been captured and had received the medical treatment he needed. He would become a Prisoner of War (POW) and survive the frightening experience of his terrible wound and the bailout at 24,000 feet. Against all odds, every crew member except Campbell lived to tell the incredible story of Red Morgan's heroic actions on board *Ruthie II*.

Red by Ruthie II. *Courtesy of Sam Morgan*

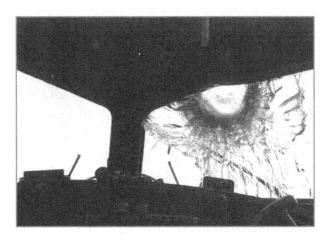

Red's Shattered Windshield.
Courtesy of 92nd USAAF/USAF Memorial Association

CHAPTER 5

Aftermath

When the story of *Ruthie II* got out, there were a lot of people scratching their heads on a number of issues. How was Campbell able to survive for several hours with such a horrific head wound? Medical personnel at RAF Foulsham determined the pilot had no chance of survival after the attack, even if he had received immediate medical attention. They did not understand how the 20 mm shell didn't kill him instantly. Red was asked about the trauma of seeing such a terrible injury to his pilot; he replied that he didn't have time for the trauma because he was suddenly busy trying to save the aircraft and crew. Morgan's epic struggle with Campbell during the mission was clearly visible the following days after the mission. Suffering multiple hits from Campbell's strong arms, the blows loosened his teeth and blackened both of his eyes. Ponte remembered Red being black and blue "from his head all the way down to his waist." Red commented afterwards that Campbell "was a big old strong Mississippi boy who didn't know he was dead."

The punishment from Campbell that Red suffered begs

the question as to why the young copilot didn't take actions to neutralize Campbell after the attack, so he could fly the aircraft unhindered. He certainly could have pulled the oxygen mask from Campbell's face, causing hypoxia and rendering him unconscious. But he knew this would probably also mean certain death for his pilot. "I just couldn't do it," he said. Another question involved the crew members in back being able to survive at high altitude (24,000 feet) with no oxygen. Climbers who attempt to scale high mountains such as Everest (29,000 feet) normally need 40 – 60 days to acclimate to the lack of oxygen. The crew did not have this luxury of time, and nobody had a plausible explanation for the miracle that occurred in the rear of *Ruthie II*. In 2012 waist gunner Ponte reflected on the gunners' survival saying, "I don't know how we survived." The crew in back did not escape totally unscathed. When Ponte passed out, he fell onto the floor, disconnecting the electric cord to his heated flight suit. When he regained consciousness, Ponte removed his gloves and discovered his fingers were frozen up to the knuckles. Suffering from severe frostbite, this mission would be his last.

II

PROBABLY THE MAIN QUESTION INVOLVES THE OTHER CREW members who were still conscious yet somehow didn't realize the crisis Red was dealing with in the cockpit. As mentioned earlier, Koske did not notice anything unusual about the performance of the aircraft, thinking any abrupt maneuvers were normal combat evasive actions by the pilots. It is understandable that once the traumatic experience with Weaver was over, he would return to his position to do his job. It would be the same thing for Irwin. His machine gun was one of only two weapons providing firepower against the continuing German attacks, and he would have no reason to leave his position and abandon that critical responsibility. With the interphone out, Red had no way of asking anybody on board for help, so he had to go it alone.

Red never blamed anybody on board for not coming to his aid sooner. He thought the crew members in back had bailed out. He found out after the mission they were unconscious, so he realized either way they could not have helped him. He was aware that Weaver was hit and in very bad shape and that Koske was totally occupied with trying to save the gunner's life. Red also knew that Irwin and Ford were at their positions doing all they could to protect the B-17 from enemy attacks. He clearly understood why he did not receive any help for over two hours.

<hr />

III

IN THE INCIDENT INVOLVING KOSKE AND WEAVER, KOSKE would later receive criticism for willingly handing over an American Airman to the enemy. Ponte would recall that "a lot of people didn't think it was the right thing to do…you don't give your wounded to the enemy." Koske had doubts in his own mind about whether he did the right thing, doubts that would remain for decades after the war ended. Although it is indisputable that Koske was the one primarily responsible for getting Weaver out of the aircraft, the decision to take that action is not as clear. A number of newspaper articles reported that it was Red who ordered the bailout. This was impossible because Red was totally consumed with maintaining control of the aircraft, and he had no way to communicate with

Koske and Weaver. Red always credited Koske for making the decision, a decision he knew was the right one. "Koske made a decision that took guts and brains—and which saved the life of Tyre Weaver…There ought to be some medal for what Koske did."

Koske himself would not take sole credit (or blame, unfortunately) for the decision. In a letter to Weaver's parents in December 1943, Koske addressed some negative comments about the bailout that were printed in the press. The comments greatly distressed Koske and he feared they would upset Weaver's parents even more. The specific comment most disturbing to Koske was "that Sergeant Weaver was thrown out of the airplane despite his pitiable protests." This was simply not true and Koske explained how Weaver clearly supported the bailout. "There was no way by which we could communicate to one another orally since the interphone was dead and we were at high altitude, but he caught my eye once, and with his good hand (the right one) he pointed towards the escape hatch."

In hindsight, it is clear the bailout was the only chance to save Weaver's life. Weaver's family certainly had no problem with the decision. His father, Tyre C. Weaver, Sr., expressed his joy in a letter to *Cosmopolitan* magazine in 1943. "The boy who was thrown out to the Germans was my son, Tyre C. Weaver, Jr., and we are glad to announce to you…that he is safe and in a German prison camp." After first hearing the story of what happened on *Ruthie II*, Weaver's family assumed he could not have survived. "We're so happy to know that he's at least alive. When the story first came out, we figured he was done for, and so did our friends. Seems like we almost have him back again, just knowing where he is and that we can send him little things."

After the war, Ponte would contact Weaver from time to time, but neither of them knew Koske's location. It wasn't until decades later that Ponte learned from Red that Koske was living in Denver and that he still struggled with what happened with Weaver on that fateful day in 1943. Ponte contacted Weaver and asked him if he was interested in a reunion with the man who had saved his life. Weaver certainly did and Ponte contacted Koske and arranged the meeting. In July, 1979, 36 years after the *Ruthie II* mission, the two were reunited in Colorado. Ponte had accompanied Weaver and remembered the smile on Koske's face when he saw Weaver. "It was like the weight of the world being lifted off his shoulders." Koske and Weaver would continue to meet in the years ahead at 92 BG reunions and other *Ruthie II* gatherings.

L to R Weaver, Ponte, and Koske Reunited.
Courtesy of Gene Ponte

Daniel Simmons

IV

ANOTHER CONTROVERSIAL ISSUE IN THE PRESS INVOLVED the coverage of Robert Campbell's condition after the attack. Many published articles that covered the *Ruthie II* story had the cruel headline that included the "headless pilot." A prime example of this came from International News Service journalist Bob Considine, who would become best known for co-authoring the books, "Thirty Seconds Over Tokyo" and "The Babe Ruth Story." Considine used "Headless Pilot" in his headlines and reported in his articles that "the head of the pilot had been blown off..." This must have been painful for Campbell's family to read, and it infuriated Red every time he saw it. He never missed an opportunity to tell anyone who would listen that this was a terrible, insensitive, and untrue statement about Campbell.

V

ALTHOUGH THERE WERE THESE CONTROVERSIAL, AND AT times conflicting, stories about the July 26 *Ruthie II* mission, the one thing everybody agreed on was that Red Morgan had done something very special. For him to fly the bombing mission with his right hand on the controls and his left hand fighting off Campbell, and then to make it safely back to England, was clearly an incredible and heroic accomplishment. The story quickly spread through military channels and it was clear Red should be nominated for the Congressional Medal of Honor (MOH). The MOH is the nation's highest and most prestigious personal military decoration that may be awarded to recognize U.S. military service members who distinguished themselves by acts of valor. Nobody could dispute that Red qualified for this medal by his unbelievable performance on *Ruthie II*.

As the story hit the newspapers, because Red had listed his parents' address as now being New York City, correspondent Considine mistakenly assumed that was Red's hometown, even though he had never lived there. According to S.A.L., Considine described Red "as a rich man raised in the lap of luxury, living in a swank apartment house..." Red was very upset by all the publicity he was receiving, and he was particularly disgusted at the false information describing him as a rich man from New York City.

There was not much action for Red as the MOH nomination made its way through military and political channels. In September 1943, the 92 BG was busy with its move from RAF Alconbury to RAF Podington in Bedfordshire. During this time Red received orders to visit every General officer in his chain of command, including Major General Ira C. Eaker, Commander of 8th Air Force (the major command responsible for all bomber units in England) and General Henry "Hap" Arnold, Commander of all U.S. Army Air Forces. The fact that Red had to visit the top Army Air Force generals indicated his approval for the MOH was simply a formality. In his folksy Texan way, Red shared the experience with S.A.L. in a letter, saying, "I never saw so many higher-ups in one day in my life. It is nice to see the ones who run this Army." In November, the MOH was official as Secretary of War Henry L. Stimson signed the certificate awarding the medal to Red. Father S.A.L. shared the contents of the certificate with the press, noting that Red was only the second living man in the European theater to receive the award. The certificate from Stimson read:

To all who shall see these presents, greeting:
This is to certify that the President of the United States
of America pursuant to acts of Congress approved
March 3, 1863, and July 9, 1918, has awarded in the
name of Congress to Flight Officer John C. Morgan,
Army Air Forces, United States Army, the Medal
of Honor for conspicuous gallantry and intrepidity
involving risk of life above and beyond the call of duty
in action with the enemy on a bombing mission over
enemy-occupied continental Europe, 26 July, 1943.
Given under my hand in the city of Washington this
29ᵗʰ day of November, 1943.

The actual presentation of the MOH to Red occurred on December 18, 1943. Eaker, now a lieutenant general, presented the medal to Red at 8th Air Force Headquarters in London. The actual MOH citation read as follows:

For conspicuous gallantry and intrepidity above and beyond the call of duty, while participating on a bombing mission over enemy-occupied continental Europe. Prior to reaching the German coast on the way to the target, the B-17 airplane in which 2nd Lt. "Red" Morgan was serving as a copilot was attacked by a large force of enemy fighters, during which the oxygen system to the tail, waist and radio gun positions was knocked out. A frontal attack placed a cannon shell through the windshield, totally shattering it, and the pilot's skull was split open by a .303-caliber[2] shell, leaving him in a crazed condition. The pilot fell over the steering wheel, tightly clamping his arm around it.

---

2   Later accounts, including Red's comments in his interviews, claimed it was a 20 mm shell.

Morgan at once grasped the controls from his side and, by sheer strength, pulled the airplane back into formation despite the frantic struggles of the semiconscious pilot. The interphone had been destroyed, rendering it impossible to call for help. At this time the top turret gunner fell to the floor and down through the hatch with his arm shot off at the shoulder and a gaping wound in his side. The waist, tail and radio gunners had lost consciousness from lack of oxygen and, hearing no fire from other guns, the copilot believed they had bailed out. The wounded pilot still offered desperate resistance in his crazed attempts to fly the airplane. There remained the prospect of flying to and over the target and back to a friendly base wholly unassisted. In the face of this desperate situation, Morgan made his decision to continue the flight and protect any members of the crew who might still be in the ship and for two hours he flew in formation with one hand at the controls and the other holding off the struggling pilot before the navigator entered the steering compartment and relieved the situation. The miraculous and heroic performance of Morgan on this occasion resulted in the successful completion of a vital bombing mission and the safe return of his airplane and crew.

On December 18, 1943, John "Red" Morgan, from Amarillo, Texas, officially became a national hero.

VI

THE WORD "MIRACULOUS" IN THE FINAL SENTENCE OF THE citation said it all. The citation reads like a fictitious Hollywood movie script rather than something that actually took place. As it turned out, the story would end up in a popular Hollywood movie in 1949. The movie "Twelve O'Clock High," based on author Beirne Lay, Jr.'s book by the same name, starred Gregory Peck, and was a story about Army Air Force B-17 crews who flew daylight bombing missions against Germany. Although the movie's story was fictitious, many parts of the screenplay were based on actual events that occurred in the European theater. At the beginning of the movie is a B-17 that belly-lands (no landing gear) at a base in England. The copilot of the aircraft, Lt Jesse Bishop, comes out of the aircraft and appears to be clearly shaken by what happened during the mission. The crew notifies the ground crew there is an arm on board, belonging to a crew member who bailed out. The pilot is in serious condition and is rushed to the hospital. During mission debrief, details emerge about what the copilot had done, details that were basically verbatim from what Red had done.

As it is with all Hollywood movies, although the story was based on Red's actions, the facts were altered for a more sensational effect. *Ruthie II* did not do a belly landing; the crew was able to lower the landing gear. From all accounts, Red did not come out of the aircraft visibly shaken. He kept his professional demeanor, understanding that he had survived a horrible ordeal but maintaining an attitude that he had just done what he was trained to do. Regarding the arm left on board, Weaver's arm did not remain on *Ruthie II*; it was dangling in his flight jacket when he bailed out. In addition, the movie depicts Bishop being so distraught he was unable to attend the mission debrief. Again, this was not something Red would do. The rest of the story of Bishop in the movie deviates from fact and ceased to have anything else to do with Red.

The great honor of receiving the MOH presented a problem for Red. For most crew members, completing 25 missions was the ticket to go home, but receiving the MOH was also an automatic permit to leave the war. After Red received the medal, General Eaker asked him what he wanted to do. Red replied, "I'd like to stay over here, General." Eaker responded by asking him why he wanted to stay rather than go home. "I like it over here," Red said. Eaker gave in and replied, "All right, but no more flying." MOH recipients were considered national heroes and it would be a tragedy if one stayed in the action and was killed. When Eaker said, "No more flying," Red said nothing. It wasn't long after this encounter that General Eaker moved on to Italy to become commander of the 15th Air Force. His replacement was General Jimmy Doolittle, the man who had led the first raid on Tokyo in 1942 and a MOH recipient himself. No longer under the watchful eye of Eaker, Red thought there might be a way for him to somehow get back into the cockpit. That opportunity came when the 92 BG transferred Red to the 482 BG, another B-17 unit that was operating out of his old 92 BG airfield in Alconbury.

General Ira C. Eaker presenting the Medal of Honor to Red.
Courtesy of Sam Morgan

Red wearing his Congressional Medal of Honor.
Courtesy of Sam Morgan

Red received by the Queen of England after his Medal of Honor mission. At his right is Prime Minister Churchill's daughter; on his left is Princess Elizabeth. Courtesy of Sam Morgan

Red being interviewed after his historic mission.
Courtesy of Sam Morgan

Daniel Simmons

Reunion circa 1987 at
Strategic Air Command Headquarters, Nebraska

L to R Maj Gen E.G. "Buck" Shuler, Mrs. Ponte,
Gene Ponte, Keith Koske, Mrs. Weaver,
Tyre Weaver, Vicki Morgan, Chris Morgan,
Red Morgan, Sam Morgan
Courtesy of Gene Ponte

CHAPTER 6

Shootdown

--------------------------------- I ---------------------------------

Everybody in the 92 BG knew the unit had explicit orders preventing Red from flying combat ever again. During Red's transfer to the 482 BG, that important piece of information was never passed on, or if it was, was never acknowledged or realized. Red obviously did not volunteer the information, just like he didn't tell the Canadians or the 92 BG that he was classified 4-F for his neck injury. For Red, just like it had been ever since he saw that first aircraft at age 4 in Vernon, it was all about the flying. When he realized he was going to be a pilot again, this time with the 482 BG, he shouted "Hot Dog!" In an interview late in his life, Red told the story of meeting General Eaker after the war where Eaker told him, "If I had known you were flying again, I would have court-martialed somebody."

In December 1943, several months after Red arrived at the 482nd, S.A.L. received word that Keith Koske, navigator on the MOH mission, had completed his required 25 bombing missions and had returned home. S.A.L. always expected (and wanted) Red to come home after his MOH mission. Talking about Red, S.A.L wrote, "I hope he gets loose and comes on home, as I feel he has faced his part of the hell through which these boys are going…If he successfully completes his 25 flights without being wounded, he will have received about all that the law of averages can do for him, and sooner or later one of his flights will bring him to grief…" Perhaps S.A.L. had a premonition, and although Red was thrilled to be flying again, he probably later wished he followed the General's orders and stayed on the ground.

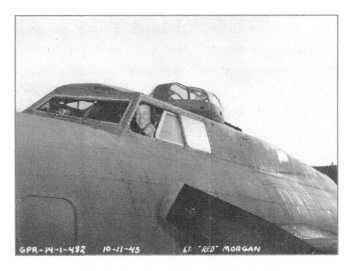

Red in the cockpit of his 482 BG B-17.
Courtesy of Sam Morgan

The 482 BG had a special mission in the air war against Germany. The unit was known as the Pathfinder group, equipped with air-to-ground radar, the latest technological invention to assist the bombers in locating their targets. While enemy fighters and flak never stopped the B-17s from completing a mission, weather was another story. Many missions were cancelled, aborted or recalled due to poor weather conditions either en route or over the targets. The 482 BG, with its new radar, enabled the crews to "see" through the clouds and effectively bomb targets in all weather conditions. As a result, the 482nd would lead the way for other B-17 groups who were not equipped with the new air-to-ground radar.

On March 4, 1944, the 482 BG led the first daylight bombing run over Berlin. Two days later, on March 6, the group would return to Berlin, this time with Red flying in the lead aircraft. The pilot was Major Fred Rabo, one of the squadron commanders in the 482 BG, and his job was to lead the 4th Combat Wing of the 3rd Air Division to the target at Kleinmachnow in the southwest corner of Berlin. There were a total of 12 on board for this mission, including Brigadier General Russell Wilson, commander of the 3rd Air Division.

As Red's B-17 began its bombing run over Berlin, it was hit with three bursts of anti-aircraft flak. Anti-aircraft flak from the Germans involved 88 millimeter artillery shells used against both aircraft and tanks. One of the shells hit the number 3 engine, setting it on fire. The other shells impacted the aircraft, which soon engulfed the B-17 in fire. It was obvious to all members on board that the bomber was not going to make it. As the flyers attempted to escape the doomed aircraft, it suddenly exploded. Red would later recall that he was conscious that something terrific had happened to his aircraft noting that "fire was all around me." He was not wearing his parachute, and just before he was blown out of the exploding B-17, with his hand he reached out and grabbed his parachute. He was now free-falling from 24,000 feet, trying to don his parachute as he tumbled through the freezing air over Berlin.

Red's parachute had been on the ramp, or "catwalk" area between the two seats, and he would later say that "he was not really sure how he got it." As he fell through the sky over Berlin, he held his parachute tightly under his arm, at first afraid to move it. He knew, however, that his only chance to survive was to somehow don the chute before it was too late. As Red struggled to get the chute on as he freefell 20,000 feet, the ground was coming up fast. He finally managed to don the parachute at the last minute—only about 400 feet in the air—and pulled the ripcord. He was so close to the ground that he only oscillated once before hitting the top of a 40-foot tree and then bouncing to the concrete below in the middle of Berlin. He hit the hard ground stiff-legged, jamming his back and knees as well as hurting his neck, injuries that would remain with him the rest of his life. The Germans arrived almost immediately after Red's hard landing, and his role in the air war had come to an end. Red would learn later that Maj Rabo had also landed safely and been captured, along with two other members of his crew. The eight remaining members of the crew, including General Wilson, were killed in the violent explosion of the B-17.

II

THE GERMANS TOOK RED TO A BUILDING SOMEWHERE IN the middle of Berlin. That night he and the other captives could hear the British bombers on their night raids over the city. The prisoners were actually safe from the attack, being held a couple floors below ground level. He had been in the aircraft for five hours enroute to the target and had a strong need to urinate. About his very personal "emergency," Red said, "I was dying!" A German soldier finally took Red outside so he could relieve himself. The German soldier cocked his rifle. "I thought he was going to shoot me but he didn't."

Red wasn't sure what was going to happen to him, understanding that going to a POW camp was probably his best option at this point. It didn't take long for the SS (abbreviation for Schutzstaffel, the foremost agency of security for the Nazis) to arrive to move the captured Americans out of Berlin. The SS took Red through Berlin, showing him the extensive damage he had allegedly done to the city. Red did not speak German, and although some of the Germans spoke English, most of them just kept pointing their fingers at the bomb damage and back to Red and the other prisoners.

The Germans took the captives to Frankfort for interrogation. During questioning of Red, the interrogator was not pleased that he was not getting any useful answers. The German told Red that he could make him talk. Red then responded with a defiant, "Go ahead." The interrogator began yelling loudly and Red thought for sure he was about to be beaten. Instead, he was placed in a very small room. One by one other prisoners joined him, to the point that they were all crammed against each other. Nobody spoke, fearful the Germans would gain information and afraid of what was going to happen to them next. The fear subsided somewhat when the captors brought in bowls of soup and allowed them to take showers afterwards. They also passed out Red Cross parcels before placing the men in a rail boxcar. The boxcar was very cold and they ended up staying there the entire night, sitting on a hard bench on one side of the train while German guards sat on the other. The next morning the train moved out, heading for what Red assumed would be a prison camp in either Germany or Poland.

III

RED WOULD EVENTUALLY END UP IN A PRISONER CAMP known as Stalag Luft I, located in Barth, Germany, and situated near the Baltic Sea approximately 150 miles north of Berlin. Although Red's interviews and all the writings about him only mentioned Stalag Luft I, he spent a very short time in another camp before being transferred to Barth. According to retired U.S. Air Force Lieutenant Colonel Irving Baum, Red was initially taken to Stalag Luft III, located in Zagan in occupied Poland, some 100 miles southeast of Berlin. Baum knew Red from their time together in the 92nd Bomb Group at Podington. Baum, a bombardier in the 92nd, was also shot down and was held prisoner at Stalag Luft III, arriving two days after the camp's famed "Great Escape" attempt. Baum saw Red one day and was happy to see somebody else who used to be in the 92 BG. He said he spent the next eight days walking around the perimeter of the camp and talking to Red about old times in the 92nd as well as their personal lives and families back home. During this short period, however, the word began to spread that the Germans were moving Red and a handful of other officers to Stalag Luft I. Baum and other prisoners in camp, including Red, did not know the reason for the transfer. Speculation was the Germans made a mistake at the outset, but Baum said it could have been for a number of reasons, including transportation issues or a realization that the prison at Barth was more secure. In any event, Red left Poland for Stalag Luft I in Germany, where he would stay for the remainder of the war. Red Morgan was the only Medal of Honor recipient to be held prisoner of war during WW II.

While Red was "safe" in a POW camp in Germany, nobody back home knew that. During WW II, it could take

60–90 days for families to find out whether their shot-down loved ones had survived and whether they were being held as prisoners. The public announcement that Red had been shot down and was missing in action (MIA) hit the newspapers on March 20, two weeks after the incident. The word first came out via United Press war correspondents and published in the New York *World Telegram* and other large-circulation newspapers. The smaller newspapers in Texas picked up the story and published it the following day.

Accounts in the initial articles quoted a crew member in the aircraft next to Red's as seeing his B-17's wing on fire between two engines, "and the plane came right back under us, so close we had to pull up to avoid a collision." Accounts also indicated the aircraft appeared to be "still under control" when it slid into the haze. For S.A.L. and the rest of Red's family, this latter report gave them hope that somehow the red-headed Texan had once again survived a catastrophic event.

Prior to the story hitting the press, S.A.L. had received official word from the War Department that Red had been shot down and that his fate was unknown. S.A.L. also received a letter from the chaplain in 8 AF Headquarters on March 14, offering "whatever of sympathy I can in this great burden." The chaplain confirmed in his letter that 8 AF did not know whether Red had become a POW. On March 29 S.A.L. wrote a letter to his sister, Margaret, notifying her that he had received no further details from the War Department. He wrote, "While the suspense is terrible, we are all cling-ing to the hope that he is safe. It will be many weeks, if not several months before we know just what occurred." S.A.L. would receive scores of letters during the following months from friends and associates expressing concern over the fate of Red. Some of the letters addressed the real possibility that Red did not survive the shootdown, which probably added to the extreme anxiety S.A.L. and Verna were experiencing. In one letter, the writer, after mentioning "the perhaps death of John Carey…," finished his correspondence by stating, "You and Mrs. Morgan have the consolation that you have come as near giving birth to an immortal as anybody who has lived on earth." It almost did seem as though Red was immortal, surviving the July 4 and MOH missions, but everybody wondered if there could possibly be a third miracle for Red and his family.

IV

BACK IN ENGLAND, CREW MEMBERS IN THE 482ND QUICKLY found out that something bad had happened when Red's aircraft didn't return. Knowing that Red had received the MOH, they knew this was not one of the "normal" shootdowns they had, unfortunately, experienced all too often. Talking about the missing pilot, the squadron's operations officer stated, "I think Red was the best-liked pilot at this base. He didn't wear his medal very much. He just didn't like to have people ask him questions about it. He was a great guy." At Podington, the home of Red's old 92nd unit, the word spread quickly. Irving Baum, who had not yet flown his fateful mission where he would be shot down, remembered when he heard the news. "The buzz was, Oh my God, Red got shot down."

On May 19 S.A.L. received a letter from the Chief, Casualty Branch, at the Army Air Forces Headquarters. Unfortunately, there was still no information about Red's status. The letter probably gave S.A.L. some hope though, as it stated, "five or six parachutes were seen to leave the disabled craft as it was descending." There were no further reports from crew members in other aircraft in the formation, so the Headquarters said there was no other information available. "The great anxiety caused you by failure to receive more details concerning your son's disappearance is fully realized." The General Officer closed the letter by assuring S.A.L. the Army Air Forces would notify him immediately upon receipt of additional information. As it turned out, the notification would come from Red himself.

On June 14 S.A.L. received a letter from Red, written on March 9, three days after the Germans captured him. It took more than three months to arrive, but S.A.L. and his family finally had the news they hoped and prayed for. Red wrote just a short message, "I am O.K. and perfectly safe. Don't worry. I will write a letter as soon as I am allowed. Love, John." It didn't take long for the word to leak out to the media as newspaper articles almost immediately spread the good news about this American hero. I am sure S.A.L.'s exuberance had something to do with the "leak" to the press. The official notification of Red's POW status did not come from the military until June 29 in the form of a telegram, with the report coming via the International Red Cross.[3] Red was alive, and that was the only thing that mattered. It did appear as though miracle number three did actually happen, but he was still a prisoner in a hostile land.

---

3   After the war, Red told the story of how his sister, Sally, a U.S. Navy Intelligence officer during the war, knew for months that Red had survived and was in a POW camp, but due to security restrictions, she could not tell their parents.

CHAPTER 7

Prisoner of War

──────────── I ────────────

With Red's journey from Stalag Luft III in Poland to Stalag Luft I in Barth, Germany, he settled into the life of a POW along with the approximately 10,000 captives in camp. The Germans did not initially realize they had captured an American Medal of Honor recipient. According to Red, the Germans normally had great intelligence on American POWs they captured. They would check graduating class rosters from the U.S., where they were able to garner background information on the individuals. Since Red trained with the RCAF, the Germans had an American prisoner with no records in the U.S. military system. It is likely the Germans did not know who they had until the media began releasing reports that he was missing. When the Germans did find out, Red did not notice any change in the treatment he received. He remained in the same barracks throughout his internment and was treated like any other prisoner.

From all of Red's accounts, it didn't seem so bad being a POW in Germany—nothing like the horror stories coming out of Japanese camps. The prisoners had their daily routines and some of them were assigned jobs to do in camp.

Red became the "coffee chef" for the Americans, something that his mother found hard to believe. Verna wasn't at all surprised that he survived the fiery plane explosion and was a POW, but she "widened her eyes" at the news of his job in camp. "Why, he never cooked at all. Maybe he's learned since he left home." Despite the relatively tolerable life in a German POW camp, that did not mean Red was satisfied with his status and that he would not find trouble with his German captors.

Chef Red. Courtesy of Sam Morgan

Red tried to escape twice, the key word being "tried." On both occasions the Germans placed him in solitary confinement for 21 days. As only Red could view his misfortune, he did not consider being locked up all alone as too bad of a punishment. He related that solitary was good because "we finally had some privacy." These incidents were rather minor and fairly commonplace among prisoners during the war.

Another incident, a much more serious one initiated by Red, would place his life in danger one more time.

—— II ——

On September 28 Red, who was living in Barracks 5 ("The Box," as he referred to it) was in another building (Barracks 1) consuming homemade alcohol, and he became intoxicated. Another POW, 1st Lieutenant Richard H. Read, who lived with Red in Barracks 5, heard he was drunk and proceeded to Barracks 1 to escort him back to their building before lock-up time. Due to Red's intoxicated state, he didn't think it was lock-up time and Read was having trouble persuading him to return to their barracks. It was approximately eight o'clock in the evening, and the accounts of the Americans and the German sentry on duty would differ as to what happened next.

The sentry claimed he locked the door to Barracks 5 and then noticed a POW climb out a window and start to move away from the barrack. The POW the sentry ended up confronting was Red Morgan. The sentry moved towards him and Red began displaying a hostile behavior. According to the sentry's account, Red "suddenly adopted a threatening attitude towards him, with clenched fists, took up a boxing stance." The German felt Red was making obvious preparations to rush at him, so he drew his bayonet. Red was not able to attack the sentry because five POWs jumped out of the barracks window and restrained him.

The story of the POWs conflicts with the German's, as they all remember that Red never made it to Barracks 5 before the incident. Red and Lt Read were approaching Barracks 5 when other POWs saw from the latrine window that Read was having trouble getting Red to cooperate. One of those POWs, 2nd Lieutenant George Davidson, jumped out of the window to help Read, which was probably the individual the sentry saw come out the window. The Americans claimed the German then "mistook Lieutenant Morgan's playful attitude" and reached for his weapon. Read stated "about six feet separated Morgan and the guard…" Davidson realized he and Read would have trouble getting Red into the barracks and rushed to the window to call for additional help. Two more POWs responded, and they carried Red and pushed him through the window and into his bed. A short time later, the sentry returned with additional men and a guard dog, arresting Red and leading him to a detention cell. At this point, Red did not resist, simply asking to take additional clothes and cigarettes. There he would await court martial charges for attempting to attack a superior.

Red believed he could possibly face the death penalty if convicted of the most serious charges he faced. As the court martial began in December, the main issue was whether Red did actually attack the German guard, who claimed he "drew his bayonet as protection against this threatening attack." The defense counsel thought it necessary to have testimony from three of the American POWs to clarify the facts which were contradictory to the guard's statement. The German legal official denied the request, but the defense counsel still collected sworn statements from three of the witnesses to present in court. Red also provided his sworn statement about that night, saying he had no intention to attack the guard, understanding those actions would have resulted in harsh punishment. "I was drunk as I had imbibed some "home-made" alcohol. I had prepared this alcohol myself out of German potatoes and jam. For this reason, I felt sick of stomach later on when I was under arrest."

As it turned out, the death penalty was probably never a possibility. The court proceedings revealed the most severe punishment for a bodily attack against a superior was imprisonment for not less than six months. For the lesser offense of threatening a superior with the committing of a crime or offense, the punishment was "severe arrest" of not less than 14 days or imprisonment in fortress arrest. Red ended up getting convicted of the lesser offense, and with his imprisonment prior to the court martial, was in solitary confinement for a total of 41 days. Even if he had been sentenced to six months in prison, he would not have stayed there for that long as the Allies were advancing quickly on Nazi Germany.

III

As 1945 began, it became more and more evident the war would end soon. American and British forces were advancing quickly from the west while the Russians were closing in on the eastern border of Germany. In the spring the POWs could hear the Russian guns as they pounded German defensive positions. The prisoners observed a noted change in the behavior of their German captors as they must have known the end was near. In the camp, while the Germans were preoccupied with preparing to evacuate, the POWs began digging ditches so they would have a place to hide when the shooting started. As the Russians approached the camp on April 30, the Germans tried to get the POWs to leave the camp, but they refused. The German guards left, leaving the POWs—mostly Americans but also Brits and Canadians—to greet the Russians. Red remembered the arrival of Russian troops and despite the camp's liberation, had nothing good to say about them. Red recalled the Russians being ruthless, killing any remaining Germans and "they shot a few of ours too." He would say later, near the end of his life, "I have no use for the Russians still."

In any event, the camp was liberated, and the POWs prepared for their return home. Red's job, along with approximately 50 other American Airmen, was to proceed to a nearby airfield and prepare it for arrival of U.S. aircraft. The incoming B-17s from England would be tasked with carrying the Americans to Camp Lucky Strike, a staging area near LeHavre, France, where they would wait for the trip back to the United States. The operation to transport the Airmen out of Germany was named "Operation Revival" and began on May 13. The B-17s were completely stripped of any equipment and armament to allow as many Airmen as possible to fit inside. This also meant there would be no parachutes for the approximately 30 passengers in each aircraft. Red would later reflect on the absence of parachutes by saying "I would have hated to spend 15 months in a POW camp and then get killed on the way to France." It only took 3 days for "Operation Revival" to remove all of the former American POWs from Barth.

Red did not take a direct route home from France. In July he was seen at a luxury hotel in Bournemouth, England. The American Red Cross had taken over a number of luxurious hotels on the picturesque cliffs on the coast of England. Many of the guests were liberated POWs, and Red was one of them. The guests at the luxury hotels reportedly paid 20 cents a night for a room; the normal charge was 10 dollars.

Completing a total of 25 and one-half combat missions (the one-half mission being the shootdown), Red had come a long way, defying death multiple times, surviving a POW camp, and now enjoying freedom well earned. His war was over, ending one of the most extraordinary, and clearly unmatched, heroism stories not just of WW II but in all of American warfare.

Red and Major Fred Rabo.
Courtesy of Sam Morgan

Epilogue

---------------------------------- I ----------------------------------

Red's life after the war was not particularly remarkable, but perhaps only when compared to his incredible experiences during the war. It was a tough act to follow. With his passion for flying, many thought he would pursue either a career in the Air Force or as a civilian pilot, but this was not the case. During his brief time in Stalag Luft III, he shared his post-war plan with Irving Baum, and his plan did not include flying. According to Baum, Red talked about having a job where he was "really needed." He told Baum that everybody drove a car and everybody needed gasoline; he talked about running a service station. Red believed this is where he was needed and, more importantly, this would allow him to settle down in one place—in either Oklahoma or Texas.

Although Red did not end up owning a gas station, he did have a career in the fuel business. He returned to Texaco in 1946, working for the vast majority of his time as an aviation representative in their sales department. His dream of settling down in either Oklahoma or Texas was never realized, as his Texaco assignments took him to New York City, Miami, Indianapolis, Minneapolis, Denver, Chicago and Los Angeles. Besides aviation representative, his Texaco positions advanced to Assistant Sales Director for Aviation (1971), U.S.A. Manager for the International Aviation Sales Department (1975), and finally Division Manager, International Aviation Sales Department—Los Angeles (1977). Red retired from Texaco on September 1, 1979.

Red did retain a relationship with the Air Force in a Reserve status, rising to the rank of lieutenant colonel. During the Korean War he was recalled to Active Duty, where he served as Deputy Assistant Secretary of the Air Force. He made every effort to fly combat missions during the war, but General Hoyt S. Vandenberg, Air Force Chief of Staff, would have no part of that. Vandenberg's decision was due in large part to what happened to America's "Ace of Aces," Richard Bong. Bong, a fighter pilot, had the most enemy aircraft kills during World War II. After the war he became a test pilot for the Air Force and was killed in an aircraft crash in 1945. The U.S. could not risk the chance of losing another national hero.

As for Red's personal life, after the war he had a brief elopement marriage to Irene Peck from New York City. After returning to work with Texaco, he would then meet the love of his life. Gladys "Chris" Ziegler was a secretary working at the Texaco office in Chicago. Red and Chris married in 1947, a marriage that would last until Red's death in 1991. They had one child—son Sam was born in 1952 and went on to have a career in the U.S. Air Force. It must have been an interesting Air Force career for Sam, being the son of an unparalleled legend and incomparable hero in military aviation.

Gladys "Chris" Morgan. Courtesy of Sam Morgan

II

RED WAS NEVER A WILLING HERO AND OFTEN FELT EMBAR-
rassed by all of the attention he received after the war. Over
the years, portions of his story were told over and over again
in Texas newspapers, Texaco publications, Air Force heritage
documents and alumni magazines from schools he attended.
His fame after the war made him a regular on invitation
lists to parties, formal functions, military ceremonies and
memorial dedications. Although he was duty-minded and
would attend many of these events, he usually avoided being
a guest speaker, not wanting to call attention to himself. At
Fairchild Air Force Base near Spokane, Washington, the "Red
Morgan Center" is a large building where the base holds award
ceremonies, promotion parties, recognition ceremonies and
heritage festivals. The base is the home of the 92nd Air Refueling Wing, the unit that evolved from Red's WW II 92nd
Bombardment Group. Because of his incredible humility, I
suspect Red would have been uncomfortable having a facility
named after him. Later in his life he reflected on his heroic

actions and the attention he so often shunned. "I have great respect for the others who have the Medal (Congressional Medal of Honor), but I really don't think about it for myself. I'm very proud to have it. Many good things have come to me because of it...But I don't dwell on the past. Frankly, I think it would be boring for people to hear about it."

Red was wrong. His story is anything but boring.

John Cary "Red" Morgan died of a heart attack on January 17, 1991, in Papillion, Nebraska, at the age of 76. He is buried in Section 59 at Arlington National Cemetery.

Red was in demand for high-level events and
social gatherings after the war.
Courtesy of Sam Morgan

Daniel Simmons

Enjoying good times with friends.
Courtesy of Sam Morgan

Remembering the fallen at a memorial ceremony.
Courtesy of Sam Morgan

The Red Morgan Center, Fairchild Air Force Base, WA
Courtesy of 92 ARW Historian

John Cary "Red" Morgan, 1914–1991
Courtesy of Sam Morgan

Author Notes

I

When I first heard the story of Red Morgan's Medal of Honor mission, I was somewhat stunned. I had watched the movie "Twelve O'Clock High" many times and was very familiar with the Lt. Jesse Bishop segment, but I thought that was just Hollywood. This could not possibly happen in real life. When I looked into Red's life further, I saw the July 4 mission where he earned the Distinguished Flying Cross. That story in itself is almost unbelievable. And then when I read about his shootdown mission, where he was blown out of the aircraft and fell three miles trying to don his parachute, I realized this was no normal human being. This man had super powers. As a military historian, I read a lot of stories of heroism in the air, and I was particularly familiar and impressed by the MOH stories. Nobody's story comes even close to what Red's experiences were during WW II.

For somebody who was never supposed to fly, John C. Morgan sure made a lot of history doing just that. It is easy to focus on his heroics in flight and in the POW camp, but I am always drawn to one incident that defined his character in my mind. After Red received the Medal of Honor, General Eaker gave him the chance to leave the war and go home. Instead, he wanted to stay. He had nothing else to prove after completing one of the most incredible flights in American history. It seems to me that being one of "America's Greatest Generation," Red rose to the top of that special group. Red was a humble man who shied away from all the attention he received after the war. When I met with Irving Baum, who knew Red when they were both assigned to the 92nd Bombardment Group, and then were reunited at Stalag Luft III, he emphasized over and over again the humble nature of Red. According to Baum, "Red's story was the greatest story the 8th Air Force has ever had. But you would never know the star of that had anything to do with it…Of all the people to receive this honor (MOH), I'll bet you he is the most modest person to ever be awarded that medal." I had the opportunity to interview Eugene Ponte in 2012, who was the only member of the MOH mission still alive. There was no doubt in Ponte's mind that he owed his life to Red Morgan. "It was an unbelievable thing he did. Not only did he bring the aircraft back, he brought back nine of us flyers with him." Red Morgan was a true American hero.

Eugene Ponte, February 2012

Daniel Simmons

This hero obviously exemplified the traits of a tough guy, but Red also had a softer side. In a Christmas interview with *The Denver Post* in 1961, he told a poignant story of his Christmas in 1944 in the German POW camp. He remembered approximately ten German youngsters coming up to the barbed wire fence singing Christmas carols for the captives. He recalled the sad looks on their faces when the armed guards made them leave. Red was touched by the children bravely approaching the camp offering songs of peace on earth to the "enemy." This tough American hero was also a sensitive, caring, decent man.

II

When I became the civilian historian of the 92nd Air Refueling Wing (successor to the 92nd Bombardment Group) in 2005, I was fascinated by Morgan's story. Red was the only Medal of Honor recipient in the history of the 92nd, yet when I was on active duty with the Air Force in the 92nd, I never heard of him. Shame on me for not researching the history of my unit, and shame on the wing leadership for not telling me. As the historian, I made it my goal to ensure that all future members of the 92nd would know the story of Red Morgan.

The 92nd Air Refueling Wing is stationed at Fairchild Air Force Base near Spokane, Washington. There was nothing on base to commemorate the heroics of this pioneer member of the 92nd. The 92nd wing commander at the time was Colonel Paul Guemmer, and when I approached him in 2011 with the idea of naming something on base after Red, Colonel Guemmer offered his full support. Colonel Guemmer's successor, Colonel Brian Newberry, was totally enthusiastic about the idea as well. All of the roads on base had already been named after great American Airmen. There were no buildings on base that sufficed to be named after a 92nd hero. The only option was to wait for a new building, one that could honorably carry the name of Red Morgan.

Fairchild AFB had a consolidated club, meaning that it was open to all ranks. The days of having separate clubs for officers, non-commissioned officers, and airmen had long since passed due to financial constraints. "Club Fairchild" was losing money every year and it closed in 2009. After several years the Fairchild AFB leadership decided to turn the building into an events center, where the wing would hold its major events, including award ceremonies, promotion parties, recognition ceremonies and heritage festivals. On June 6, 2014, Colonel Newberry, on behalf of the 92nd Air Refueling Wing, dedicated this building as the Red Morgan Center with Red's family members in attendance. Red's portrait of his MOH presentation and his story hang proudly in the entrance to this events center. Everyone coming into the 92nd will know the name and the heroics of John Cary "Red" Morgan.

III

I TITLED THE BOOK "WITH HIS HAND" FOR SEVERAL REASONS. The obvious one is that with his hand he fought off the mortally wounded pilot, with his hand he controlled the B-17 through the bombing run, and with his hand he grabbed his parachute as he was blown from his exploding aircraft. But it is also a reference to somebody else's hand. My research did not uncover whether Red was a particularly religious man. But in an interview, he acknowledged that he must have received help from above for him to have survived those catastrophic events. I truly believe the hand of God played a role in Red's survival.

80   *Daniel Simmons*

During that same interview, Red was asked if he panicked when he was blown out of his B-17 and freefalling while not wearing a parachute. Red responded, "Twice in my life (MOH mission and shootdown) I knew I was dead, so under those circumstances you don't panic. If you know you're dead, that's it. It's the uncertainty that frightens you..." I related to that, because it has always been the fear of the unknown that has caused me the most stress.

My intent in writing this book was not to provide a history of strategic bombardment in WW II, or the history of the 92nd and 482nd Bombardment Groups, or to talk about the details of operating the B-17. There are many books on these issues, written by much better authors than me. My intent was to tell the story of Red Morgan. This was simply an attempt to combine all of the information I had obtained on this incredible man, because I considered this the greatest story never told.

Colonel Brian Newberry, 92nd Air Refueling Wing Commander, and Sam Morgan unveiling Red's Medal of Honor portrait. Fairchild Air Force Base, WA, June 6, 2014 Courtesy of 92 ARW Historian

Colonel Brian Newberry and Red's Family Members,
Fairchild Air Force Base, WA, June 6, 2014
Courtesy of 92 ARW Historian

Daniel Simmons

*Portrait of Red Receiving the Medal of Honor, displayed in Red
Morgan Center
Courtesy of 92 ARW Historian*

APPENDIX A

References

Books

The Route as Briefed by John S. Sloan, 1946, Argus Press.
92nd Bomb Group (H) Fame's Favored Few by Dave Turner with Robert D. Elliot, 1996, Turner Publishing Company.
The Mighty Eighth in WW II—A Memoir by Brig. Gen. J. Kemp McLaughlin, USAFR (Ret.), 2000, The University Press of Kentucky.

Documents

TWENTY-EIGHTH MISSION OF THE 92ND BOMB GROUP, 4 July 1943, Air Force Historical Agency Archives, Maxwell AFB, AL, Reel B0181, PDF Page 1945.
THIRTY-SIXTH MISSION OF THE 92ND BOMB GROUP, 26 July 1943, Air Force Historical Agency Archives, Maxwell AFB, AL, Reel B0181, PDF Page 1960.
Record of Service, Morgan, John Cary, R109911, Royal Canadian Air Force, 1 August 1941.
Attestation Paper, R.C.A.F. Form R. 100, Royal Canadian Air Force, 6 August 1941.
Record Sheet, Morgan, John Cary, R.A.F Form 1580, Royal Air Force, 23 March 1943.
Parchment Certificate of Discharge of John Cary Morgan, Royal Canadian Air Force, 23 March 1943.
Data Pertaining to the Court Martial of 1st Lieut. John C. Morgan, Stalag Luft I, December 1944, Courtesy of Sam Morgan.
Texaco Employment Record for John Morgan, September 1, 1979, Courtesy of John C. Harper, Chevron Historian

Interviews

Morgan, John. Interview with Imperial War Museum, U.K., via www.iwm.org.uk. Creator Roger Freeman. Catalogue Number 30040, 1977-05-04.

Morgan, John. Personal interview (video). Interviewer unknown. Circa 1990, Courtesy of Sam Morgan.

Ponte, Gene. Interview with author (video). February 9, 2012.

Baum, Irving. Interview with author (audio). August 12, 2014.

Personal Accounts

"Ruthie I," *92nd Bomb Group, 325th Squadron, 8th Air Force,* 07-04-43, Personal Written Account by Gene Ponte, n.d.

"Ruthie II," *92nd Bomb Group, 326th Squadron, 8th Air Force,* 07-26-43, Personal Written Account by Gene Ponte, n.d.

Red Morgan Stories, Personal Written Account by Mary Tom Crain, n.d., Courtesy of Sally Thomas

Articles

Crain, Mary Tom. "Living Texan! Memories of Our Summers on the Ranch." *Accent West,* Amarillo, TX, November 2003.

Burnham, Perry. "Target – Jul 4, 1943, LEMANS-NANTES-LA PALLICE." *92nd Bombardment Group News,* Vol. VII, Letter 6, June 1983.

Frisbee, John L. "Crisis in the Cockpit." *Air Force Magazine,* Vol. 67, No. 1, January 1984.

Considine, Bob. "Bleeding to Death, This Gunner Fell 5 Miles to Germany—and Is Alive." *International News Service,* December 4, 1943.

Considine, Bob. "Texan in 'Headless Pilot' Saga Gets Medal of Honor." *Fort Worth Star via International News Service,* December 12, 1943.

Author Unknown. "Texaco's Flying Pioneer – An American Hero." *Texaco Topics Publication,* 1977.

Overend, William. "Reminiscing With Yesterday's Hero." *Los Angeles Times*, September 12, 1976.

Considine, Bob. "Four-Hour Flight Through Hell." *The Texaco Star* via *The International News Service*, Fall 1943.

Considine, Bob. "Mission Complete." *Cosmopolitan*, December 1943.

Author Unknown. "Red Morgan Coffee Chef in Prison Camp." *Amarillo Times*, October 11, 1944.

Montes, Veronica. "Team Fairchild honors Lt. John "Red" Morgan during dedication Ceremony." *Fairchild Flyer*, June 13, 2014.

Pearson, Greg. "Denverite Recalls a German Christmas—in Prison Camp." *The Denver Post*, December 24, 1961.

Letters

Koske, Keith to Tyre C. Weaver, Sr., December 16, 1943

Morgan, Samuel Asa Leland to various recipients, 1941 – 1945. See Appendix B.

Internet Sites

http://www.92ndma.org – 92nd USAAF/USAF Memorial Association

http://www.homeofheroes.com/wings/part2/08_morgan.html - Home of Heroes

http://www.cemetery.state.tx.us/pub/user_form.asp?pers_id=11035 – Texas Cemetery

http://www.merkki.com/morganjohn.htm - Stalag Luft I

https://www.thisdayinaviation.com/tag/john-cary-morgan/ - This Day in Aviation

https://www.findagrave.com/memorial/7869617/john-cary-morgan - Find a Grave: Arlington National Cemetery

https://haysfreepress.com/2018/03/07/only-medal-of-honor-winner-taken-prisoner/ - Hays Free Press News-Dispatch

http://www.482nd.org/ - 482nd Bomb Group

http://www.nmmi.edu/overview/heritage.htm—New Mexico
Military Institute

http://www.91stbombgroup.com/ - 91st Bomb Group

https://www.skylighters.org/ - 225th AAA Searchlight Battalion

http://www.gov.dod.dimoc.26506 – USAF video: "Medal of
Honor – With One Hand"

http://en.wikipedia.org/wiki/Twelve_O'Clock_High - Twelve
O'Clock High movie

http://www.tsha.utexas.edu/handbook - The Handbook of Texas
Online

http://www.327th.org/Morgan%20MOH.htm – 327th Bombardment Squadron

http://www.arlingtoncemetery/jcmorgan.htm - Arlington Cemetery

APPENDIX B

Letters from
S.A.L.

June 5, 1940.

NATURAL GAS PIPELI

20 N.

CHICA

PHONE RAN

You suggest that you hope John will not rush into uniform in the event the war situation continues to look worse. If the country becomes involved in a war of defense, I would expect him to enter the army when others similarly situated are called on to go. I don't think he will rush in as a matter of mere adventure. Had he been able to go on and qualify as an expert aviator, he might do so, just because of his love for that kind of thing; but I do not expect him to rush in just for the thrill of getting into uniform. He got over a lot of that walking area down at N.M.M.I. A uniform probably doesn't appeal to him as much as it would to one who had never worn one. Naturally, I am depressed when I think of the direction in which we are going because of these two boys, both of whom would doubtless be called on should the country become involved in a serious war. If Hitler wins and destroys the British and French empires, there will be no living on this earth with him, so far as this country is concerned, unless we are willing to swallow all that has been sacred to the country and allow him to dictate to us and cuff us around as a big bully would a small boy. We will not stand for that sort of thing, and I have no more doubt that we will be at war with him in less than three years if he wins in the present conflict than I have that the sun is shining outside.

Love to all of you,

Earl Morgan

November 10, 1941

I am glad you had a letter from John, and it pleases me to have you say you were impressed by it. I think John has settled down a great deal, and the experience through which he is passing and which he has cut out for himself are calculated to complete the job. I suppose he wrote you from his new address. If not, you may now address him: AC.2 John C. Morgan, No. 2 I.T.S., Regina, Saskatchewan, Canada, R. 109911.

Love to all of you.

r brother,

Earl Morgan

E COMPANY OF AMERICA

ACKER DRIVE

O ILLINOIS

OLPH 0278-L.D.4 II

THE TEXAS COMPANY
135 EAST 42ᵈ STREET
NEW YORK

February 23, 1942

We have not heard from John for two or three weeks. I am expecting him to complete his course at Virden, Manitoba, any time now, and he expects to have home leave for a few days after his course is completed. I am going to have him come over to New York and visit us during that leave.

Love to all of you,

NATURAL GAS PIPELINE COMPANY OF AMERICA

20 N. WACKER DRIVE

CHICAGO. ILLINOIS

PHONE RANDOLPH 0278-L.D.4 II

August 4, 1941.

John has joined the Canadian Air Force. I took him to Windsor, Canada, yesterday a week ago, and he was promptly accepted as an applicant for a pilot's commission. His address is now Royal Canadian Air Force, c/o Manning Depot #2, Brandon, Manitoba, Canada, where he will be for the next eight or ten weeks. After about five months of training he expects to go across to England, by which time he will probably see plenty of action. He is taking a very serious step; but thirty years ago, had I been confronted with the same situation, I would have done likewise. He just couldn't see going into one of these draftees' camps as a private and spending an indefinite period marching around through the mud or dust and carrying a rifle or a broomstick and going through the same calisthenics through which he went for 3½ years in military school. You probably know that he has done a lot of amateur flying. That experience together with his military training ought to put him in line to make rapid progress toward his commission.

Love to all of you,

Your brother,

May 11, 1942

When he visited us the latter part of February he was disappointed because he would not be permitted to go on and qualify for the acrobatic or fighter service, in which there is only one man to a plane. He didn't want the bomber service. Fortunately, while here in New York he met a Major in the American air force who very patiently undertook to get him straightened out. He emphasized the fact that the bomber service is after all the more important, because the fighter goes out to protect the bomber while the latter does the real work against the enemy. He answered John's argument that he didn't want to go up in a bomber where he would be at the wheel with the responsibility for the lives of several other men, or where he would be in the crew and have his own life in the hands of the pilot. He wanted to be responsible for his life alone, and wanted the opportunity to save his own life through the exercise of his own judgment if he got into difficulties. The Major told him that he thought it was an added protection to his own life to be responsible for the lives of others - he would be more careful - and the same would be true of another pilot who was responsible for his life should he happen to be at the bomber releases rather than at the plane controls. I think he feels better about it. He is now frightened, however, over the prospect of being made an instructor rather than getting to go across. There is such accelerated necessity for the training of pilots that they are going to have to use a lot of these boys who have finished the courses as

instructors for those who are just entering the service. This is true both in this country and in Canada. He has had a wonderful course up there, and from what I hear about it, it is even a tougher course than they have been giving in this country.

Sam will be coming over in a few weeks at the close of the session in Northwestern. I don't know whether he will attend summer school here or whether he will get out and work during the vacation. He will do one or the other.

Verna and Sara are fine. I think Verna is planning to go over to Evanston and return with Sam. They may bring John's car back over here.

ORGAN & BRITAIN

ERS

R-EAKLE BUILDING

TEXAS

TH FLOOR
ORTY-SECOND STREET
K. N. Y.

John's present address is:

Morgan, J.C.   R 109911
No. 16, Service Flying Training School
Hagersville
Ontario, Canada.

Don't be offended if he doesn't answer your letters as promptly
as you think he should. He doesn't write to us, and Sam is
even worse than he is. We have had one letter from Sam since
we came over here.

Love to all of you,

August 8, 1942

You probably know that John is still in Hagersville,
Ontario, where he is well along toward the end of his training
course. He has his 150 solo hours in the air and lacks only
the completion of his exacting courses in the higher branches
of mathematics, including navigation, before he will be turned
out a full-fledged pilot. He is discouraged over the fact that
he will probably be assigned to an instructorship in some of
the training camps instead of being sent into combat service.
I can sympathize with his disappointment, though I consider
it a distinct compliment to him that he would receive such an
assignment. They have so many hundreds of thousands of flying
cadets to put through the training courses that it is essential
that they assign a great number of the older men to the job of
training the recruits. I think that work is just as important
as the combat work, since it is one of the essential activities
necessary to the winning of the war.

Lots of love,

October 31, 1942

TWENTY-FC
ONE THIRTY-FIVE EAST
NEW Y

Your letter to Verna, which came in this morning, reveals that you had learned that John has left for England. He got his wings on October 9th and on the same day was given his orders to report to the R.C.A.F. at Halifax on October 24th. He was given a furlough so that he could come home in the meantime. He left here on the 21st and we have not heard from him since. He is not permitted to let us know when he is leaving, of course. We will probably not hear until he gets to England and then he won't be permitted to tell us where he is. He looked fine when he left, though he came home with a terrible cold and had it most of the time he was here. He finally got into the fighter service. He was determined to do that. It has both advantages and disadvantages, and I am not sure whether I would rather see him in that branch or in the bomber service. He was determined to fly and it may be that he will be just as apt to come through it alive manipulating his own plane as he would if he were on a bomber with a whole crew. In any event, that is what he wants, and far be it from me, if I could do so, to try to map out his course in this war.

Lots of love,

January 2, 1943

There is nothing of any particular interest at this end of the line, except that we have heard from John several times since he has been in England. In his last letter he stated that he is now with the R.A.F. and is in the bomber service. Indirectly we heard through the family of the boy who went over there with him that he was in the hospital in November, but John said nothing about that. I suppose it was some temporary trouble with his bronchial tubes, which have been bothering him since he went up to Canada. I am hopeful that they will transfer him to the North African scene so that he can get away from the bitter, damp climate of England. I suppose he would be in nomore danger down there than he will be piloting planes in the fogs around Britain. He was making a final effort to get into the American Air Force at the time he wrote us last. I hope he succeeds, as I would rather have him in the American Air Force, particularly since he is doing the work of a commissioned officer and I would like to see him commissioned.

Lots of love,

Daniel Simmons

URTH FLOOR
FORTY-SECOND STREET
ORK, N. Y.

February 12, 1943

We had a letter from John this week and he seems to be getting along fine. He is a bomber pilot, though he is again trying to get on a fighter plane. I don't think he will get away with it, however, as he has passed the age limit. Sam has not been called.

Lots of love,

Sa L Morgan

March 26, 1943

Sarah is supposed to get her commission in about three weeks. Sam is here on his between-term vacation but will return to Northwestern Sunday. He goes into uniform July 1st and doesn't know where they will send him for further training. I had a cable from John indicating that he feels fairly certain that he will be transferred to the American Air Force. He has been working on this ever since he went over there and I hope it goes through.

Love to all of you,

Sa. L. M.

June 23, 1943

We had a letter from John last week but he said nothing that was of any particular interest except that he is getting along well and is happy with his present assignment. He is pretty much put out about the coal strike and expressed a desire to see John L. Lewis take about three flights over Germany, which he thinks will permanently cure him of his tendency to strikes.

Lots of love, *your Brother,*

Sa L Morgan

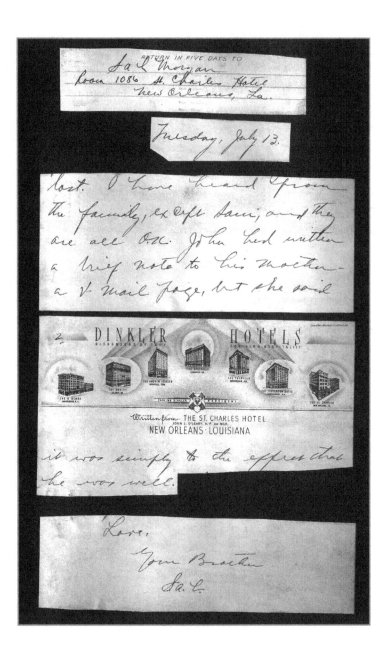

RETURN IN FIVE DAYS TO
Sal Morgan
Room 1086 St. Charles Hotel
New Orleans, La.

Tuesday, July 13.

last. I have heard from
the family, except Sam; and they
are all O.K. John had written
a brief note to his mother—
a V mail page, but she said

DINKLER HOTELS

Written from THE ST. CHARLES HOTEL
JOHN J. O'LEARY, V.P. AND MGR.
NEW ORLEANS · LOUISIANA

it was simply to the effect that
he was well.

Love,
Your Brother
Sal.

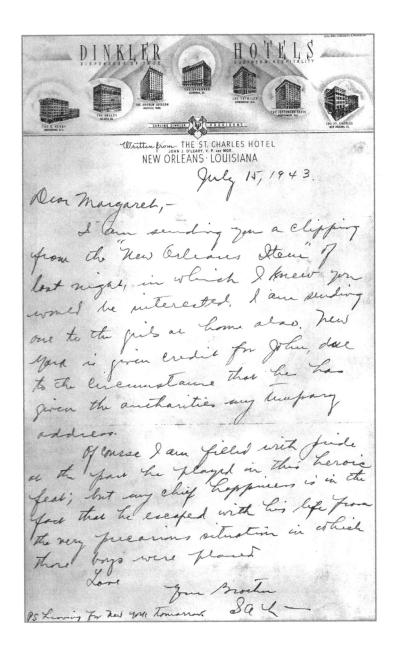

Written from THE ST. CHARLES HOTEL
JOHN J. O'LEARY, V. P. and MGR.
NEW ORLEANS · LOUISIANA

July 15, 1943.

Dear Margaret,—

I am sending you a clipping from the "New Orleans Item" of last night, in which I knew you would be interested. I am sending one to the girls at home also. New York is given credit for John, due to the circumstance that he has given the authorities my temporary address.

Of course I am filled with pride at the part he played in this heroic feat; but my chief happiness is in the fact that he escaped with his life from the very precarious situation in which those boys were placed.

Love
Your Brother
S. A. L.—

P.S. Leaving for New York tomorrow.

TWENTY-FOURTH FLOOR
ONE THIRTY-FIVE EAST FORTY-SECOND STREET
NEW YORK, N. Y.

July 30, 1943

Dear Sisters:

Herewith I hand you a clipping from this afternoon's
edition of the New York World Telegram, from which you will
see that John has already had another hairbreadth escape. It
looks from this as if John is thoroughly capable of assuming
the title of pilot in lieu of his former title of co-pilot.

One of the boys on the wrecked plane which was
brought back on July 4th, who lives in Jersey City across
the river from New York, wrote his mother that it was the
Texas pilot who brought that plane back, observing in that
connection that he was regarded by his associates as one of
the best pilots over there.

Love to all of you,

_J. a. L._

August 19, 1943

Mr. Morgan dictated the enclosed letter when he
expected to have extra copies of the paper containing the
clipping. He was not able to get them, so the Editorial
Department had the one clipping photostatted. It is
certainly a wonderful article but I am sure not a surprise
to anyone who knows John.

Sincerely yours,

August 12, 1943

Dear Sisters:

Herewith I hand you a clipping from the Nashville Tennessean showing a feature store by Bob Considine, correspondent for the International News Service, who is now in England, concerning John's recent exploit over Germany.

The fact that John gave my address as River House, New York, caused the reporter to let his imagination run wild, as you will see from the article, in which John is described as a rich man raised in the lap of luxury, living in a swank apartment house and running with the Stork Club set. As you will infer from the fact that I live there, all those who live in River House are not rich and living in the lap of luxury. John never lived there and he was never in the Stork Club in his life.

This story has been published all over the country and it has almost made John a national hero. How he went through this experience without losing his life I shall never understand.

Love,

S a L

September 4, 1943

I received the editorial and cartoon from the San Antonio Light which Margaret sent me from Temple. I appreciate this very much. It is a matter of very profound satisfaction that an exploit of John's could be used with such effect as the San Antonio Light has used this one. I wrote the editor explaining that Considine was in error in stating that John lives in New York, and of course I pointed out that he is a Texas boy, born at Vernon and reared at Amarillo.

Love to all of you,

J. a. Y. M

TWENTY-FOURTH FLOOR
ONE THIRTY-FIVE EAST FORTY-SECOND STREET
NEW YORK. N. Y.

September 11, 1943

Dear Margaret:

I have your letter of Wednesday with enclosure of
the clipping from the Fort Worth Star Telegram, and also
your letter addressed to me at the hospital. That is a
picture of John which I have had on my desk here ever since
he left. I can't imagine where the press got hold of it
unless it came out of Canada.

John's story must have been published all over the
United States. We have received clippings from different
places, including one from a Palo Alto, California, paper.
It was also published by the Canadian papers, due to the
circumstance that a man up there happened to know that he had
been a member of the Canadian air force. The story is going
to be published in the Texaco Star, a magazine circulated
among the Texas Company employees, and this will be an illustrated
story. I will send you a copy when it comes out. The Cosmopolitan Magazine sent a man over to get some information concerning John and stated they were going to carry the story in
an early issue.

We had a letter from John yesterday. He is terribly
put out about the publicity his feats have received, and seemed
to be especially peeved because they referred to him as a soft,
rich fellow who spent his time running around with the Stork
Club set. I don't know whether he is mad because he thought
that sort of representation reflected on him or whether he is
mad because instead of living that kind of a life he was driving
a truck for the Texas Company down at Oklahoma City before
entering the air corps. He was disgusted also because the
stories all gave him credit for living in New York, where he
says he never lived and never expects to. Those boys have a
code of ethics among themselves that they are not to boast
of their achievements or exploits, and I have an idea that
John feels like he might be blamed by his fellows for all this
publicity. As a matter of fact, it was his shipmates who put
the news out. He had nothing to do with it.

I am returning the clipping as per your request.

Love to all of you,

Jay

TWENTY-FOURTH FLOOR
ONE THIRTY-FIVE EAST FORTY-SECOND STREET
NEW YORK, N. Y.

September 25, 1943

Dear Sisters:

I have time for just a brief note to advise
that the New York Times this morning carries an item
headlined Washington showing that John has been decorated
with the "Bronze Oak Leaf Cluster to Air Medal." As I
understand it, this is a double decoration, the first being
the Air Medal and the Oak Leaf Cluster being the additional
decoration instead of a second Air Medal. Naturally, I
am very happy about this. I knew you girls would be
interested in knowing about it if it is not carried in
your local paper. It may not be, for the reason that his
address is still shown as New York.

I will write you a longer letter sometime soon.

Love,

Ja. L. M

P.S. You might check with the "Times" and
see if they caught this item.

October 23, 1943

TWENTY-FOU
ONE THIRTY-FIVE EAST F
NEW YO

    The address you have of John is not sufficient,
I am afraid. His correct address is:

```
F/O John C. Morgan    T190641
482 Bomb Grp.  (P)  813 Sqd.
A.P.O. 634
c/o Postmaster
New York, N.Y.
```

    You have his old A.P.O. number, and it may be that
his letters will be forwarded to him. They should have been
returned to you unless they were going on to him. I have
written him today and in the letter inquired as to whether he
has been receiving your letters and whether he got the package
you sent him.

Love to all of you,

November 4, 1943

Dear Sisters:

    You will be interested in looking at the
December Cosmopolitan, in which, beginning at page 44,
is another story about John. It is too bad they had to
throw in all that bunk about his being brought up in a
rich man's home, with nothing to do but to decide whether
he would have steak or chicken, etc.; but aside from
that it is a very good story.

Lots of lov

October 26, 1943

I had a letter from John yesterday, from whi
quote two or three paragraphs:

"A couple of weeks ago I was called to head
and told to report to wing headquarters. I went down
commanding officer and found that I was wanted by Gen
Williams. Went in to see him and he told me that a r
my trip had been read to an assembly of high air forc
including General Arnold and General Eaker. He congr
me and all that bunk.

"The next day I received orders to report t
Anderson and went there. I went in and had a talk wi
got the same old stuff and was told that General Chau
wanted to see me. They furnished me with a private c
proceeded cross country to General Chauncey's headqua
got the works, and learned that I was to report that
General Eaker so kept the car and proceeded to his he
Went in to see him and he said that he just wanted to
and congratulate me and that General Arnold wanted to
same. I then went in to see him. Sat down and had q
with him. He was very nice indeed, as was General Ea
the rest. Anyway, I never saw so many higher-ups in
my life. It is nice to see the ones who run this arm

It is nice to know that his superiors clear
to his Four-Star General have taken notice of his ach
Nothing in John's letter indicates that he is the lea
puffed up about it. I suppose the experiences throug
went took care of that.

Love to all of

S. a. L.

We have heard from John once since I wrote
. His letter was written on October 11th. They have
some pretty extensive air operations over the Con
ent since that time, in some of which he probably has
ticipated.

December 15, 1943

TWENTY-FOUR
ONE THIRTY-FIVE EAST FO
NEW YORK

We have not heard from John for nearly a month. Somehow I have a notion that he may be showing up here most any time. He will be grounded automatically upon the completion of 25 flights over enemy territory but will have the privilege of applying for another assignment of five flights. His command will then pass on whether or not he will be permitted to do that. I expect him to make the application, as he has such a dread of being brought back here to become an instructor. He prefers to be in the thick of it.

The boy, Koske, who was mentioned prominently in the various stories covering the second mission is back in this country. This would indicate that he has completed his 25 flights. It may be, however, that John has not completed as many as Koske for the reason that he injured his arms and knees in both the July 4th flight over France and the July 26th flight over Germany. That may have kept him from going on some expeditions in which Koske participated. I hope he gets loose and comes on home, as I feel that he has faced his part of the hell through which these boys are going, at least for a while. If he successfully completes his 25 flights without being wounded, he will have received about all that the law of averages can do for him, and sooner or later one of his flights will bring him to grief, so I hope he won't be too stubborn about returning to this country and taking up more safe if less glamorous activities.

Verna is about as usual. She has been busying herself with some Christmas shopping for Sam and the three girls. She sent John's packages several weeks ago.

Love to all of you,

TWENTY-FOURTH FLOOR
ONE THIRTY-FIVE EAST FORTY-SECOND STREET
NEW YORK, N. Y.

December 23, 1943.

Dear Sisters,-

Miss Swanson is away, so I'm writing just a note. You may have seen where the ceremonies in connection with the award to John of the Congressional Medal of Honor occurred in London last Saturday. We heard the whole thing over short wave, on invitation from British Broadcasting Company. Among other things there was a short talk by John which did him great credit.

The New York papers have full of praises for his heroism, and I think every one of them has carried his picture.

We are going to talk to him by radio Sunday afternoon over the "Army Hour" about 2:30 P.M. your time. Thought you might wish to listen in. Please tell Fannie and Mr. and Mrs. Henry Hobbs. Can't write them all by long hand. Have had the flu again, and Verna has gone down with it. Sarah has a terrible cold, but has managed to stay on duty, which happened to be from 12 o'clock midnight to 6 am this week. In writing John don't mention our being sick. We'll be well before he hears it, and he is faced with enough without worrying about us.

Merry Christmas to all of you and to Waldo.

So L

January 17, 1944

ONE THIRTY-FIVE E.

I have yours of last Wednesday, which I did not receive until today. I am sorry I did not receive it in time to be on the lookout yesterday afternoon for the dramatization of the book "Target Germany."

I am enclosing some extra clippings referring to John, which I hope will help out in the scrapbook you are preparing for him. I have not received your clippings but they will doubtless be here in a day or two. You probably sent them regular mail.

There is no news since I wrote you last. We are on a rather routine program and nothing of interest happens. We have not heard from John for about a month. Somehow I have hopes that he will be showing up here one of these days for an extended furlough, though I have no basis for such hope.

Love to all of you,

P.S. John has a new number. His address now is:

        Lt. John C. Morgan 0-2044778
        482 Bomb Grp. (P) 813 Sqd.
        A.P.O. 634
        c/o Postmaster, New York, N.Y.

January 24, 1944

I have your note added to the letter of Miss Frankie Mae Webb dated January 14th, in which she asked for a picture of John. We will have one available in a few days but do not have one available now. I have written her to that effect as per enclosed copy. I will send the Fort Worth Star Telegram one of the same pictures.

Love to all of you,

Daniel Simmons

APPENDIX B

FOURTH FLOOR
ST FORTY-SECOND STREET
YORK. N. Y.

January 24, 1944

Miss Frankie Mae Welborn, Business Manager
Texas Student Publications, Inc.
University Station
Austin, Texas

Dear Miss Welborn:

My sister, Miss Margaret L. Morgan, 1602
Fillmore Street, Wichita Falls, has forwarded to me
here your letter of the 14th instant, in which you ask
for a good picture of Lt. John C. Morgan, my son, for
use in the Cactus.

We have recently received the negative of a
good picture of him taken at London the day of his
decoration and we are having some pictures struck from
that negative now. As soon as they are delivered I
will send you one. I wonder if you would like to have
a copy of the citation supporting the award and also
the certificate of the award, both furnished me by the
War Department?

Yours very truly,

SALM.S

TWENTY-FOURTH FLOOR
ONE THIRTY-FIVE EAST FORTY-SECOND STREET
NEW YORK. N. Y.

March 6, 1944

The day that John went down

Dear Margaret:

I have yourw of the 29th enclosing a copy of London Calling containing a story about John. We received a copy of the same paper from John about the time you received yours, so I am sure John sent the one to you. I immediately had the one I received phostatted and mailed you a copy of the photostat. If that photostat will answer your purpose, I would like to keep the paper you sent me, since I took the original home for the scrapbook they are making up there. I intended to have another photostat made from the negative for John's file here in the office. If you prefer to have the paper, however, I can have another photostat made and return this paper to you. Let me know which you would rather have.

I am not sure whether you have heard that John has been promoted to a first lieutenancy. From another source I have learned that he is only making one combat flight out of four in which his squadron is sent across. The remainder of the time he is spending in operations, and when he completes the limit of his flights he will be assigned to operations altogether. This, I think, will be a splendid experience for him, looking ahead to his future.

Love to all of you,

J. a. C. Morgan

APPENDIX B

March 29, 1944

Second letter after news of John

Dear Margaret:

I received your letter with the several enclosures. I am returning the script of the radio program and the letter from the advertising company as per your request. We made a copy for John's file.

We have no information in addition to that appearing in the papers as to John's misfortune over Berlin. We have official confirmation from the War Department that he has been missing since March 6th, but there are no details. We also had a letter from Lt. Helene J. Lieb, of the ANC, a friend of John's about whom he has written us. She wrote us on the 11th that she had been down to John's base and talked to the boys who saw his plane go out of formation, and all reported that his plane appeared to be under control when it disappeared from view, and all were confident that he and the other members of the crew either put the plane down or parachuted to safety. Captain Berkowitz, a former roommate of John's, who came back to this country about two months ago after completing his maximum number of flights, called up by long distance telephone from Atlantic City to reassure us with the observation that there was no better flying team in all England than John and Major Rabo, and that he had no doubt that nothing worse had happened than that they had been made prisoners of war.

While the suspense is terrible, we are all clinging to the hope that he is safe. It will be many weeks, if not several months, before we know just what occurred. It is very helpful to know from telegrams, letters, telephone calls, and personal calls that there are so many of his friends and our friends who are pulling for him in their hopes and prayers.

Love to all of you,

Dad.

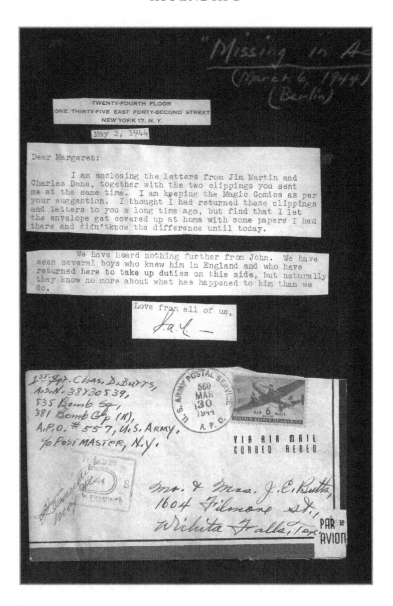

Acknowledgments

First and foremost, I want to thank Red's son, Sam, for all of the information and photos he provided. His three scrapbooks were "pure gold," especially the letters in them that were written by Red's father, S.A.L. Red's niece, Sally Thomas, provided wonderful information on Red's early life, as documented by her mom (Red's sister) Mary Tom Crain. I had no anecdotal information on Red's life as a child until Sally shared Mary Tom's personal accounts. Irving Baum, who passed away in 2014, was an invaluable source for information on the 92nd Bombardment Group and also for his accounts of the personal relationship he had with Red both during and after the war.

Other contributors I am thankful for include Jim O'Connell, 92nd Air Refueling Wing Historian; Duane Wolfe, President of the 92nd USAAF/USAF Memorial Association; the Air Force Historical Research Agency; Canada's Library and Archives; and John Harper, Historian at Chevron Corporation.

I would also like to thank Paul Guemmer and Brian Newberry, former commanders of the 92nd Air Refueling Wing, for their support in dedicating the Red Morgan Center on Fairchild Air Force Base.

Of course, I wish I would have had the chance to meet Red. He has given me the greatest military aviation story I know. During my research I also developed a great respect and admiration for his father S.A.L. I wish I could have met him, too. His letters during the war enabled me to separate fact from the fiction which was often reported in the newspapers. Thank you, Red, and thank you, S.A.L.

Finally, I have to thank my wife, Wendi, for her unfailing support during this labor of love. Her dogged encouragement made the difference in me finally completing this project.